The Project on
European-American Relations

Relations between Western Europe and the United States have become more turbulent in recent years. Divergences in interests and perceptions have grown. Many are questioning the fundamental assumptions of the postwar period. There is a broad consensus that the European-American relationship is in a state of transition.

A new generation is emerging and a number of social and cultural changes are under way that are also contributing to this transition. While our common heritage and values set limits on how far we may drift apart, there is an increasing recognition of the divergences between the United States and Europe on such critical issues as defense and arms control, policy toward the Soviet Union, East-West trade and technology transfer, West-West economic relations, North-South issues, and problems outside the NATO area. The challenge for statesmen will be to manage the differences—and where possible create a new Western consensus—in such a way as to enable the Alliance to adapt to new circumstances while preserving its basic character.

The relatively simple world of the postwar period is gone. Americans today appear to have less understanding of European perspectives and Europeans less appreciation of American views. There is much handwringing about the trans-Atlantic malaise, but less constructive thinking about how to manage and, where possible, reduce our differences.

The project is designed to identify and clarify the differences in interests and perspectives affecting critical issues in the European-American relationship, thereby enhancing understanding across the Atlantic. Approximately three issues per year will be selected for examination on a rolling basis over the next three years. The issues will be those that are most likely to create friction in the period ahead.

A short book will be published on each issue. European and American authors with points of view that differ from each other but represent important strands of thought in their respective societies will contribute analyses of the problem and offer their policy prescriptions. We hope that by disaggregating the issues in this manner, we can make a constructive contribution to the Atlantic debate.

An advisory group of Council members, with the participation of European guests, helps to choose the issues and discusses the ideas in the manuscripts prior to publication. They are, however, in no way responsible for the conclusions, which are solely those of the authors.

This is the second book in the series. The first book addressed the role of nuclear weapons in the defense of Western Europe and dealt with both military strategy and arms control.

We would like to thank the Rockefeller Foundation, the Andrew W. Mellon Foundation and the German Marshall Fund of the United States for their assistance in supporting this project.

Cyrus R. Vance

2

UNEMPLOYMENT AND GROWTH
IN THE WESTERN ECONOMIES

Andrew J. Pierre, Editor

Marina v.N. Whitman
Raymond Barre
James Tobin
Shirley Williams
Introduction by Robert D. Hormats

COUNCIL ON FOREIGN RELATIONS, INC.
58 East 68 Street, New York, N.Y. 10021

COUNCIL ON FOREIGN RELATIONS BOOKS

Printed in the United States of America

Library of Congress Cataloging in Publication Data

Main entry under title:

Unemployment and growth in the Western economics.

(Europe-America series ; 2)
1. Unemployment--Addresses, essays, lectures.
2. Economic policy--Addresses, essays, lectures.
3. Full employment policies--Addresses, essays, lectures.
4. Economic history--1971-   --Addresses, essays,
lectures. I. Pierre, Andrew J. II. Whitman, Marina
von Neumann. III. Council on Foreign Relations.
IV. Series: Europe/America ; 2.
HD5707.5.U54 1984   331.13'791812   84-9415
ISBN 0-87609-001-3

Advisory Group
Project on European-American Relations

The editor would like to thank C. Michael Aho, James Chace, Edwin A. Deagle, Jr., George de Menil, William Diebold, Jr., François Duchêne, Alan Greenspan, Anne Heald, Norman Jacobs, Sylvia Ostry, John E. Sawyer, and Peter R. Weitz for joining the Advisory Group in its discussions on this topic. He would also like to thank Pat Bridges, Andrea Giles, David Kellogg, Helena Stalson, Kathy Stotter, and Rob Valkenier for their assistance in the production of this book.

The Project on European-American Relations is under the auspices of the Council's Studies Program.

Contents

About the Authors

Marina v.N. Whitman is Vice President and Chief Economist of the General Motors Corporation. She was a member of the Economics Faculty at the University of Pittsburgh from 1962 to 1979, where she held the title of Distinguished Public Service Professor of Economics from 1973 to 1979. Mrs. Whitman served as a member of the President's Council of Economic Advisers in 1972-73; as a senior staff economist for the Council in 1970-71; and as a member of the Price Commission in 1971-72. In addition, she is currently a member of the Department of the Treasury's Advisory Committee on Reform of the International Monetary System. Her publications include *Reflections of Interdependence: Issues for Economic Theory and U.S. Policy.*

Raymond Barre served as Prime Minister of France from 1976 to 1981 and is currently a Deputy in the National Assembly. He was Minister of Economic and Financial Affairs (while Prime Minister) from 1976 to 1978; Minister of Foreign Trade from January to August 1976; a member of the General Council of the Banque de France in 1973; Vice Chairman of the Commission of the European Communities responsible for Economic and Financial Affairs from 1967 to 1972; and Director of the Office of the Minister of Industry in France from 1959 to 1962. In addition, Mr. Barre is a Professor at the Institut d'Etudes Politiques in Paris and he held the Chair of Political Economy at the University of Paris-Sorbonne from 1963 to 1976. He is the author of *Economie Politique* and *Une Politique pour l'Avenir.*

James Tobin is Sterling Professor of Economics at Yale University, where he has taught since 1950. He was awarded the Nobel Memorial Prize in Economic Science in 1981. In addition, Mr. Tobin served on the President's Council of Economic Advisers in 1961-62 and is the author of a three-volume series *Essays in Economics,*as well as *Asset Accumulation and Economic Activity (Reflections on Contemporary Macroeconomic Theory), The New Economics One Decade Older,* and *National Economic Policy.*

Shirley Williams is President and co-founder of the Social Democratic Party in Great Britain and has been a Professorial Fellow at the Policy Studies Institute in London since 1979. Previously, she served in Parliament from 1981 to 1983 as a member of the Social Democratic Party and from 1964 to 1979 as a member of the Labour Party. She was Secretary of State for Education and Science from 1976 to 1979; Secretary of State for Prices and Consumer Protection from 1974 to 1976; and Parliamentary Secretary to the Minister of Labour in 1966-67. In addition, Mrs. Williams was Chairman of the Organization for Economic Cooperation and Development's Examination on Youth Employment Policies in the United States, West Germany, Ireland and Denmark, and is the author of *Politics is for People, Jobs for the 1980s,* and *Youth Without Work.*

Robert D. Hormats is Vice President for International Corporate Finance of Goldman, Sachs & Co. and a Director of Goldman Sachs International. Previously, he served as Assistant Secretary of State for Economic and Business Affairs from 1981 to 1982; as Deputy U.S. Trade Representative (with ambassadorial rank) from 1979 to 1981; and as Deputy Assistant Secretary of State for Economic and Business Affairs from 1977 to 1979. Mr. Hormats was a Senior Staff Member for International Economic Affairs on the National Security Council from 1974 to 1977, having been on the staff earlier from 1969 to 1973. In addition, he was a member of the U.S. delegation to the Versailles, Ottawa and Venice Economic Summits and played a major role in earlier economic summits.

Andrew J. Pierre is a Senior Fellow at the Council on Foreign Relations and the Director of the Project on European-American Relations. Formerly on the staff of the Brookings Institution and the Hudson Institute, he has also taught at Columbia University. In addition, he served with the Department of State as a Foreign Service Officer in Washington and abroad. Mr. Pierre is the author of *The Global Politics of Arms Sales, Nuclear Politics: The British Experience with an Independent Strategic Force, Nuclear Proliferation: A Strategy for Control,* and other works.

Robert D. Hormats

Introduction

Full employment and vigorous economic growth have been fundamental goals of every Western nation since World War II. Yet in
the last ten years virtually all of them have experienced their highest rates of unemployment and deepest economic decline since the
depression.

Unemployment today is a major human, social and moral problem in the Western world. It poses a direct political and economic
challenge to the credibility of Western leaders and to Western
stability. Prolonged high unemployment has already been the
proximate cause in some countries of the ouster of governments
and of a weakening of support for the market system over which
they preside; and it has contributed to frictions which have jeopar-
dized the cohesion of the West. Serious domestic problems have
compelled governments to turn inward and have reduced both
their sensitivity to the effects of their policies on others and their
willingness to make short-term compromises, even when they
serve long-term interests.

Policies in one country that create unemployment, as well as
those designed to correct it, have serious impact on that country's
trading partners. Recession, high interest rates, trade protection
and subsidies on one side of the Atlantic affect jobs and economic
activity on the other. In turn, they become a source of political
contention and impair security cooperation.

Moreover, the popular disaffection that results from an inability
to create adequate numbers of jobs can reduce political support
for government policies in other areas (e.g., defense and foreign
affairs); and the cost of unemployment—in terms of lost output
and budgetary expenditures for worker compensation—reduces
resources available to the economy for other purposes. Indeed, the
difficulty governments have in finding sufficient resources to
strengthen conventional forces in Europe has been a major factor
in NATO's inability to reduce reliance on the nuclear deterrent.

1

And many of the tensions that result from nuclear fears on both sides of the Atlantic can be traced to this failure.

The seriousness of prolonged joblessness and the consequences of an inability to reduce it have not been lost on heads of state. At every Western economic summit, beginning with Rambouillet in 1975, the subject has been addressed and pledges have been made to bring about a reduction in unemployment. At the Bonn summit in 1978, leaders agreed on a common strategy for growth based on the "locomotive pull" of key economies. In other years the emphasis was on the growth, or anti-inflationary, policies of individual nations, without an agreed allocation of responsibility. But despite the best of intentions, the unemployment problem is far from resolved.

Even in the United States, where roughly 20 million new jobs were created in the last decade and unemployment has declined from nearly 11 percent to below 8 percent in roughly two years, joblessness remains very high among minority groups. It is particularly serious among young blacks and Hispanics—who suffer from an unemployment rate estimated at about 40 percent. Among young people as a whole, unemployment rates increased from 11 percent to 17 percent between 1979 and 1983.

In recent years there have also been major layoffs of experienced workers, especially in basic industries such as textiles, shoes, steel, coal and autos—with heavy concentration in the Northeast and Midwest. In part this increase is attributable to the recession, but it is also due in part to technological displacement and the permanent scaling-down of capacity in these sectors. At the same time wage disparities and barriers to access for women and minorities have diminished opportunities, incentives and the chance to obtain work experience.

Europe has experienced a similar set of problems, but in practically all respects its situation is much worse. In sharp contrast to the United States, European job creation was virtually stagnant in the 1970s. Youth unemployment increased dramatically—from just under 4 percent in West Germany in 1979 to well over 13 percent at the end of 1983; in France and Great Britain roughly 25 percent of all young people in the job market are unemployed. The duration of European unemployment is also greater than that of the United States—whereas 7.7 percent of those who were unemployed in the United States in 1982 (the last year for which

Organization for Economic Cooperation and Development figures are available) remained so for over 12 months, the comparable figures in France, West Germany and the United Kingdom were 39 percent, 21 percent and 33 percent respectively.

In June the West will hold its annual economic summit. It will present an opportunity once again to address the employment problem and the broader question of securing and sustaining economic recovery. The same issues will be confronted in the campaign leading up to the U.S. presidential and congressional elections. It is, therefore, an opportune time to take a hard look at the problems of jobs and growth. The purpose of this book is to do just that by engaging the talents and experience of knowledgeable Americans and Europeans in order to generate an enlightened debate on the subject so we can learn from the successes and failures on both continents. Our hope was and is to demonstrate that the 1980s need not see a prolongation of high structural unemployment; nor should nations be forced into the trap, once again, of sacrificing large numbers of jobs in order to reduce inflation or of solving domestic economic problems at the expense of other countries.

This book provides a fresh look at the problems of growth and employment. It is not an attempt to reach a unanimous consensus on causes or remedies. In fact, while there are several areas where views converge, there are also important differences that serve to sharpen the debate and provide a range of alternatives.

Major Points of the Authors

There is general agreement among all contributors that a major reason for high unemployment was the sharp decline in economic activity in the United States and Europe during the past decade, with the current slow recovery of Europe continuing to add to the problem. All agree as well that a sustained reduction of unemployment requires a strong and enduring recovery. But they have important differences of view, particularly with respect to Europe, as to how to bring about such a recovery and about how effective it will be in significantly reducing unemployment.

James Tobin contends that macroeconomic stimulus is "necessary" and "probably sufficient" to lower unemployment to rates comparable to those of the late 1970s and that structural labor-market policies, suggested by other contributors, can make only "marginal improvements." While recognizing that governments are frequently unwilling to adopt expansionary policies because of their inflationary impact, he believes that in the present circumstances—because of progress made in West Germany and Japan in lowering real wages and structural budget deficits and because of their high savings rates—both countries "have plenty of room for expansionary fiscal policy." To a lesser extent, he believes the same is true of Great Britain.

Calling for "international coordination" of macroeconomic policies to stimulate growth, Tobin recommends that the United States take the lead by shifting to a tighter budget and a more stimulative monetary policy, while at the same time other major economies loosen both monetary and fiscal policy.

In addition, he suggests the possibility of incentive subsidies to encourage employers and workers to agree on "compensation systems which, like the Japanese model, condition some payments to workers on the profits or revenues or productivity gains of the firm." Tobin also advocates consideration of wage-price guidelines strengthened by incentives for compliance such as penalties and rewards. These would "avoid the rigidities and inefficencies of absolute controls" while diminishing the inflationary risk of demand expansion.

Raymond Barre differs from Tobin on two major points. First, he believes that "a growing part of unemployment is structural" and feels that "the jobless cannot be absorbed into the labor market even in a period of high economic activity." Second, he is skeptical of "mechanisms for the coordination of economic policies," believing that summits and similar meetings have not "thus far created effective obligations for governments."

Arguing that the U.S. economy is more flexible than that of Europe, he cites the enormous number of new jobs created by the U.S. private sector in the late 1970s. This is compared to virtually no net new private job creation in Europe, which saw a greater increase in government employment and in part-time jobs. Barre is particularly concerned about the alarming increase in youth unemployment and the duration of joblessness in Europe—the latter being, in his view, attributable to insufficient labor mobility, the effect of very high unemployment insurance payments, and too few new employment opportunities. He is also concerned about the slowdown in investment in Europe relative to gross national product (GNP), the reduced competiveness resulting from increases in unit wage costs relative to competitors, and the decline in return on invested capital. These factors add to joblessness and hinder European competitiveness with the United States and Japan.

As may be expected in view of their different analyses of the problem, Barre's solutions vary from Tobin's in some respects, but are similar in others. They agree that European interest rates have been both forced up and held up by high American interest rates. The result has been to weaken investment in Europe and, because of the impact of such rates on the debt-service burdens of developing nations, to constrain Third World imports from Europe. And he sees the rise in the value of the dollar, while advantageous to European exports, as contributing to an outflow of capital to the United States. His great "regret" about the American international economic role is that its budgetary policy "remains in such bad shape."

Other policy concerns that Barre mentions relate to European budgets—which amount to roughly 50 percent of gross domestic product (GDP)—and the growing weight of interest on the public debt. Alarm over the size of European budgets has led to efforts to raise taxes and cut expenditures. This is intended to permit an "easing of fiscal pressure and [to] offer greater opportunities for private investment" as well as to "allow central banks" to pursue a more flexible monetary policy. It is this series of constraints on fiscal stimulus that Barre sees as dominant and, in fact, as causing "nations with a low inflation rate" to be "unable to exploit this advantage."

Barre suggests an "active policy for employment." This would include continued efforts to moderate the growth of wage costs so as to restore the international competitiveness of firms and increase their financial resources. Such a policy would also set up early retirement and pre-retirement systems to alleviate the need to fire older workers and at the same time open up opportunities for younger workers; create a carefully worked out and economically sound program for part-time work; develop policies to increase the mobility of labor; and establish programs to support small businesses.

Marina Whitman's approach falls somewhere between those of Barre and Tobin. She believes that "economic expansion could, at a minimum, reverse much of the sharp rise in unemployment during the past four years," and she points to the recent decline in U.S. joblessness as evidence. Recovery would also help to overcome structural rigidities by increasing the availability of funds to address structural problems, such as youth unemployment; and, by permitting productivity growth to exceed that of real wages for a time, thus encourage more hiring. She also shares the views of both Barre and Tobin that high U.S. interest rates and large government deficits have an adverse impact on European recovery. But in addition she cites the Organization for Economic Cooperation and Development's (OECD) call for greater fiscal stimulus in other major industrialized countries and coordination among such measures to maximize their effectiveness and minimize associated risks.

However, even before the downturn in the late 1970s, unemployment rates in the United States and most of Europe were significantly above historical postwar norms, Whitman notes. In her view, a cyclical upturn would still leave substantial structural unemployment. She sees this as due in part to the more rapid growth in real wages than in productivity and points to the benefits of recent real-wage deceleration to restore competitiveness in lagging industries.

She also examines the differences in emphasis between the European and American approaches to the structural unemployment problem. The absence of a vigorous new jobs market, an increase in the average duration of European unemployment, impediments to the mobility of labor and capital, and demographic trends that indicate that joblessness is likely to increase in the next few years lead many Europeans to focus on the "structure of unemployment and job tenure," while the United States tends to emphasize "making markets more flexible and competitive." But, she adds, many Americans and Europeans share the view that subsidies, protection and job sharing are necessary in the current environment.

Whitman believes that the best approach to structural joblessness is one which encourages increases in productivity and competitiveness. She also recognizes that new technologies require a painful transition for many and that governments must ease this pain in ways that encourage rather than retard growth. Europe needs to enhance competition, promote increased integration, improve profitability and the availability of capital to new businesses, and increase private investment. For the United States, she cites the recommendations of the President's Commission on Industrial Competitiveness, which favor improving the educational system and economic opportunity, encouraging investment in research and development, strengthening the access of new business to low-cost capital, and reducing administrative impediments to exports.

Like Tobin, Whitman calls for improved policy coordination. She stresses how important it is that governments take into account the "external effects of [their] particular mix of monetary and fiscal policies," which have a major impact on exchange rates and thus on the "transmission of economic fluctuations across boundaries." While the United States is particularly important in this process, Europe and Japan "must share the task of keeping exchange-rate relationships in reasonable alignment by paying increased attention to the effects of their fiscal, monetary and financial policies on the external value of their currencies." In a similar vein she argues for greater consistency of monetary goals to avoid "a collective excess of either stimulus or restraint in the global economy."

In conclusion, she states that we are in a period of transition moving from the "hegemonial organization of the postwar past to the more collective forms of leadership and responsibility required for the future." To deal with current problems, an " 'implicit bargain' " is required in which the United States would take "greater account of the trans-Atlantic spillover of its economic policies and curb its tendency toward 'global unilateralism,' " while Europe and Japan would "share responsibility for maintaining Western security, the viability of the international trade and financial systems, and the health of the global economy."

Shirley Williams shares Whitman's concern about the harmful political impact of unemployment as well as about the friction between the United States and Europe regarding economic and security issues. And she shares the concerns of the other contributors about the impact of the U.S. budget deficit on European interest rates and on the future international recovery. She links the deficit closely to the value of the dollar and thus to protectionist pressures in the United States and to economic frictions between the European Economic Community (EEC) and the United States.

Hope for reducing unemployment lies in services in her view, especially in those based on new technologies. She cites the phrase of one commentator who contends that the choice "may be new jobs or no jobs." Regarding the United States and Japan as well placed to take advantage of new technologies, she feels that the rigidity and greater centralization of Europe's economies impairs their progress.

She puts forward a number of specific suggestions for policy improvements on the microeconomic level including the rapid dissemination of technological knowledge, the development of flexible modern training schemes, and the education of young people in basic information technology skills. In addition, creating jobs in economic infrastructure, by rehabilitating houses and by building and improving roads, bridges and sewers, she notes, requires less capital per employee than in smokestack industries and is unlikely to be inflationary because of the relatively small firms involved.

Another important source of new jobs, according to Williams, is the "associative sector," which encompasses workers cooperatives and firms supported by government loan guarantees. Also, she advocates job sharing, flexible retirement, and a reduction in work hours as other means of creating job opportunities.

On the macroeconomic level, Williams shares Barre's skepticism about the effectiveness of economic policy coordination among Western nations. She states that "The harsh truth is that the West has not pulled itself together since the United States effectively lost its economic hegemony in the 1960s." However, she still believes, as does Tobin, that if the United States cuts its budget deficit, other Western governments should be able to pursue more expansionary policies.

A Western Strategy for Jobs and Growth

Unemployment and slow growth cause major divisions within and among our societies. It is less and less acceptable to our publics to suffer through a sharp drop in employment in order to curtail inflation, as the West has just done, or to endure a sharp increase in inflation in the name of stimulating growth, as happened in the 1970s. Moreover, democratic societies cannot afford, and should be morally committed to avoid, the alienation among the younger generation that will occur if large numbers of them cannot find entry-level jobs and become increasingly frustrated as lack of experience causes them to fall further and further behind. And the social costs of large-scale unemployment among minority groups are extremely high, especially in societies seeking to heal old wounds and broaden human opportunity.

In addition, because of the frictions caused by poor economic performance among our nations, the West needs to take a new look at how it organizes itself to deal with the problem of unemployment and growth in light of the major economic changes of the last decade. These changes are apparent in the increase in magnitude of international trade (world exports have grown from $190 billion in 1965 to $1.9 trillion in 1983) and financial flows (U.S. assets abroad grew by $4 billion in 1965 and by $118 billion in 1982). Equally significant changes have occurred in the characteristics of the world economy—for example, greater government intervention in international trade and the switch to a floating-rate international monetary system.

There are, of course, no easy answers to the problems of unemployment and growth. And this book is not intended to propose definitive solutions. But on the basis of the work of the authors, and my own experience, I believe the following ideas to be worthy of serious policy consideration.

First, Tobin makes a convincing case that another try should be made at coordinating, or at least harmonizing, macroeconomic policy. He suggests that the United States take actions to reduce its budget deficit and that others loosen their fiscal policy (which could be done through tax incentives for investment or public construction projects, as Williams and the OECD also recommend) to the degree compatible with their inflationary circumstances and ability to borrow without weakening the private sector. As the dollar weakens other countries can also afford to relax monetary policy without bringing about a weakening of their own currencies. The OECD could be useful in identifying the likely individual and collective impact of such actions taken together by several nations.

In the longer run, the OECD should be the forum for improved procedures to permit countries fully to assess and consult about planned changes in monetary and fiscal policy before final decisions are taken. This would permit each country to consider the impact of its proposed policy changes on others and in so doing to better identify the feedback or secondary effect on its own economy. To use the failure of policy coordination in 1978 as evidence that such coordination cannot now succeed does not give sufficient weight to the disruptive impact of the oil shocks that followed the fall of the Shah, which were heavily responsible for that failure.

Second, there appears to be broad agreement, emphasized by Whitman, Williams and Barre, that the preferred response to current problems is to enhance competitiveness and reduce economic rigidities. Ways of doing this include increased economic integration (e.g., lower barriers to worker mobility and investment) in Europe, improvements in both business profitability and investment incentives, and avoidance of a major gap between wage and productivity increases (which could involve greater use of the "bonus system," so that workers would obtain a share of improved profitability, and layoffs could be minimized during bad years).

In addition, ways should be found to increase availability of capital to new and small businesses. This takes on particular significance in light of the recent U.S. experience—which saw the large majority of new jobs in the 1970s created by firms under five years old and by small companies of less than 25 employees. Both the United States and Europe should make a major effort to facilitate the flow of capital to new and small businesses.

Traditional core industries could be helped by the creation of an industrial version of the Federal National Mortgage Association. This would support private lending to capital-short industries that need to introduce new technologies in order to improve their competitiveness—particularly to those that have been provided import relief or that have been injured by imports but not to the extent that they can obtain relief under existing statutory criteria.

Third, Europe and the United States need more active approaches for reducing structural unemployment. Among the most promising are:

Job Sharing. While there are some drawbacks to this approach, such as additional management and non-salary costs, it can be especially helpful in giving younger people entry-level jobs and so permitting them to gain experience; and it permits management the flexibility of having a larger number of people to call on for overtime. For older people who do not wish to fully retire all at once, or for women or men who wish to spend additional time at home with younger children, job sharing is also a desirable option. To make it attractive to employers, however, a formula needs to be found so that job sharing does not involve a net addition to wage costs, and so that attendant management and non-salary costs can be minimized.

Gradual Retirement. This approach, which could be a version of job sharing, would allow workers past retirement age, or those who wish to phase into retirement, to gradually reduce the amount of hours they work, thus making spaces for younger people and, perhaps, helping to train them as well.

Public Works Programs. Particularly in the United States, with its seriously decaying infrastructures, the need to improve roads, bridges, waterworks and sanitation systems also presents an opportunity to increase productive employment and to address a pressing national structural problem, especially in regions where there have been major layoffs in traditional sectors. While budgetary constraints will for a time limit the size of such programs, stronger emphasis on them by the federal and state governments is clearly needed. Moreover, such improvements will reduce "inflationary bottlenecks" which would otherwise occur.

Improved Education and Training. It is impossible to overstate the importance of this aspect of the jobs and growth problem. When competitive shifts within and among economies were gradual, and technological change was not so rapid, the educational system had more time to adjust, as did workers. Today's job market demands better skills and greater adaptibility than ever before, and thus emphasis on education and training *throughout* one's career to permit workers to move more easily up the job ladder or out of less promising sectors into more promising ones. A strengthening of the educational system to produce the required numbers of engineers and scientists, to equip others in society with the ability to understand and take advantage of new technologies, and to insure that high school training is relevant to the jobs of the 1980s and 1990s is imperative. And there must be a greater emphasis on continuing education and training at all levels. Creation of what have been labelled "individual training accounts" would also improve prospects for men and women to both acquire new skills and move into new jobs. (Employers and employees would deposit funds into these accounts so that if a worker is laid off, the funds would pay for retraining and/or relocation. Otherwise, the worker's deposits would go into his or her Individual Retirement Account.) Ensuring the "portability" of pensions would also facilitate worker mobility.

Fourth, equal economic opportunity is a fundamental pillar of democracy. While progress has been made in reducing barriers to employment and wage disparities for women and minorities, these remain serious problems. Moreover, they deprive our economies of the benefits of the improved productivity that these people can bring as they gain experience and are given rewards commensurate with their abilities. A number of legislative proposals have been made in the United States and Europe for improving economic equity through pension reform, day-care centers, additional training, and elimination of salary discrimination. European and American officals should exchange views on how their countries have dealt with these problems and collectively move to make improvements in these areas.

Fifth, trade and monetary issues have come to have an increasing impact on domestic employment and growth. It may not be possible soon to have another highly formal round of trade negotiations like the Kennedy or Tokyo Rounds, and indeed much damage is likely to be done in the time required to prepare for one. But the major industrialized and developing trading countries should move promptly to begin negotiating a reduction or elimination of recently imposed trade distortions. They should also act soon to develop new procedures for advanced notification prior to government intervention (e.g., subsidies, import protection, "target industry" policies); for limiting the duration of such intervention; for offsetting or reducing its impact on other countries; and for ensuring that intervention is accompanied by internal adjustment measures designed to phase it down and out as soon as possible.

Monetary issues, such as exchange-rate misalignments and volatility, also require a somewhat different approach. Because of the major impact of a country's exchange rate on its own economy and others, the effect of its monetary/fiscal policy mix on that rate requires particularly careful attention. Considerably greater harmonization of policy mixes will be required to prevent exchange rates from entering "danger zones" that lead to domestic economic and trade distortions—which in turn cause pressures for protection. If financial, monetary and trade officals could meet periodically to identify the ranges or zones of exchange rates most likely to avoid major, domestically harmful, trade distortions, and if they could identify the types of monetary/fiscal policy mixes most likely to keep currencies within these ranges and make maintenance of such ranges an important objective of economic policy, that would be a major step forward.

Sixth, collective management will be required if the world economy is to function effectively in the decades ahead. While the United States, because of the strength of its economy and the central role of the dollar, will need to play the major leadership role, others will need to join in. And the United States will need to bring others along if it expects to succeed in obtaining the changes in the trading system and other aspects of the world economy that it wants. To secure the support of others, the United States will need to be more sensitive to the impact of its policies on others, and Europe and Japan will need to be more active in promoting an improved trading system and working out a sharing of responsibilities and benefits in the areas of economic, political and security cooperation with the United States.

April 1984

Marina v.N. Whitman

Persistent Unemployment: Economic Policy Perspectives in the United States and Western Europe

Concerns about unemployment have been close to the center stage of both American and European policymaking throughout the postwar period. But at present, with the jobless rate in many industrialized countries at or near its highest level since the 1930s, the political sensitivities associated with this issue are particularly acute. The cyclical aspect of this synchronized unemployment is generally recognized on both sides of the Atlantic, although there may be some disagreements regarding its relative importance in the total problem. There are, however, important differences of view about the causes of and the cures for the structural component of joblessness—that is, the portion that would persist even at high levels of capacity utilization and economic activity.

It is important, of course, not to overgeneralize the notion of an "American" or a "European" view of the problem: Europe consists of a number of countries with heterogeneous political, economic and social environments, experiences and institutions; and in the United States opinions on these issues are far from monolithic. But this complexity does not reduce the urgency of addressing the systemic aspects of the common problem of cyclical unemployment in an increasingly interdependent global economy, nor of trying to minimize the frictions that are likely to be generated as governments attempt to act on differing perceptions of the origins of structural unemployment and the measures that might be taken to alleviate it.

In both Europe and the United States, the magnitude and persistence of the unemployment problem have produced analytical confusion and policy vacillation. The confidence of policymakers in the effectiveness of traditional Keynesian countercyclical measures has been shaken. Policies of demand stimulus, which were, for the most part, an effective antidote to high unemployment during the 1950s and 1960s, fell into disfavor in the late 1970s as spiraling inflation beset the global economy. Many countries have turned increasingly to monetary and fiscal restraint, either in direct response to rising inflation, or to protect their exchange rates from depreciation as other countries tightened their anti-inflationary policies.

The second oil shock and a sharp rise in inflation laid the foundation for the large cyclical increase in unemployment throughout the industrialized world since 1979. In the United States the underlying inflation rate spiraled upward from less than two percent in 1960 to ten percent in 1979. And, with the consumer price index— a widely publicized although less accurate barometer of inflationary pressures—soaring at a 15 percent rate in late 1979, inflation became a serious political liability. This situation set the stage for a major change in U.S. monetary policy.

In October 1979, Paul Volcker, Chairman of the Federal Reserve Board, announced that the central bank would henceforth place greater emphasis in its day-to-day monetary management on controlling the money supply and less on reducing short-term fluctuations in interest rates. This change was only one among a number of factors that contributed to a sharp rise in the unemployment rate. But it was symptomatic of a major shift in attitude. Concern about inflation had become so intense in the United States that the adoption of a less discretionary, and therefore less accommodative, monetary policy became an acceptable option. This shift in emphasis was instrumental in bringing about a greater-than-expected slowing in inflation and in pushing the unemployment rate to higher levels than it might have reached with a more discretionary set of operating guidelines for the "Fed."

Inflation has dropped markedly from its pre-recession levels throughout the industrial world and there are even some tentative signs that a more-than-cyclical reduction may have occurred. In the United States, for example, the increase in consumer prices in 1983 was some two percentage points below the 1976 rise—the cyclical trough for inflation following the mid-1970s recession. This pattern may represent a departure from the trend of upward-ratcheting inflation that has prevailed since the 1960s. But inasmuch as the most recent period of cyclical weakness was the most severe and prolonged since the 1930s, it is far too early to infer that lasting progress has been made in restraining inflation. Concern about a recurrence of severe inflationary pressures continues to dominate U.S. monetary policy.

A timely and significant easing in monetary policy occurred during the summer of 1982 in response to several highly visible bankruptcies and a sharply weakening economy. For the most part, however, U.S. monetary policy has been constrained in responding to the sharp rise in unemployment since 1979. And with a stronger-than-expected economic recovery resulting in a significant reduction in unemployment on this side of the Atlantic during 1983, and some signs that economic activity is beginning to pick up in Europe, there is little domestic political pressure for more stimulative macroeconomic policies. The principal issue of contention is whether the prospects for a sustainable world recovery would improve with a more balanced mix of monetary and fiscal policy in the United States.

The emphasis could change if the recovery falters. But with the legacy of the inflationary surge of the late 1970s hanging over decision-makers in both the public and private sectors, prescriptions for demand stimulus are no longer widely viewed as the primary remedy for high unemployment. Mitterrand's France, the only country to attempt a traditional Keynesian solution to its rising unemployment, was forced by accelerating inflation and currency depreciation to shift gears to a policy of austerity in the spring of 1983.

Unemployment: A Deep-Seated Problem

The reluctance to employ more stimulative macroeconomic policies may reflect a widespread perception that our current unemployment problems are to a significant extent structural in origin. As noted in the *1983 Economic Report of the President*, even after full recovery, a serious structural unemployment problem will remain unless measures are taken to improve the functioning of labor markets. The forecast that gives flesh to the bones of this general statement is that the U.S. unemployment rate is likely to reach a plateau of six to seven percent and remain there for a protracted period. Although there are no similarly authoritative views in Europe on the magnitude of structural unemployment, preoccupation with this aspect of the problem is even more intense there. In contrast with the U.S. economy, which created more than 20 million net new jobs during the 1970s, aggregate employment in the major West European economies was essentially unchanged during this same period and was actually lower in 1983 than in 1973.

Moreover, demographic factors and trends in female labor force participation rates suggest that there could be added pressure on structural unemployment in Europe during the 1980s. While the birth rate was declining in the United States during the early 1960s, it was rising in Europe. As a result, the teenage population in the United States began to decline in 1978, while it has only recently begun to decrease in Europe. This development suggests that an older and presumably more experienced work force will exert downward pressure on the U.S. unemployment rate into the 1990s. In Europe, by contrast, where the 20- to 24-year-old age group is still increasing, demographic factors will put upward pressure on unemployment rates for some years to come.

The European labor markets will be confronted with an even greater challenge to their job-creating capabilities if women there follow the American example. Some 53 percent of American women over age 16 are currently in the labor force, up from 37 percent in 1960. In Europe, however, the participation rates of women, with the exception of the Scandinavian countries, have risen at a much slower pace than in the United States. But the participation rates for European women are beginning to accelerate, suggesting that, as the U.S. Commissioner of Labor Statistics has noted, "The differences [between Europe and America] are primarily a matter of timing and degree."[1]

The issue of structural unemployment takes on added urgency in light of a widespread fear that, in the words of noted economist Wassily Leontief, the current wave of new technology may lead to permanently higher joblessness on both sides of the Atlantic.[2] Concerns about machines displacing human labor go back at least to the Luddite outbursts that marked the early days of the Industrial Revolution. Throughout history, apprehension and, in some

---

[1] Janet L. Norwood, "Labor Market Contrasts: United States and Europe," *Monthly Labor Review,* August 1983.

[2] Wassily Leontief, "The Distribution of Work and Income," *Scientific American,* September 1982.

cases, outright hostility have greeted the introduction of labor-saving technological advances. Such responses are, of course, predictable and understandable from workers threatened with displacement from their jobs and fearful of the premature obsolescence of their skills. But apprehension on the part of a Nobel laureate in economics is more unusual.

Leontief believes that the "electronic revolution" is qualitatively different from those that have gone before. He argues that, while previous technological advances have replaced human physical labor, electronic innovations will instead replace mental effort, threatening the human brain itself with technological obsolescence. But if past patterns offer any reliable guide, the technological revolution on which the world is currently embarking may be seen rather as the latest in Schumpeter's waves of "creative destruction," in which innovation acts as a catalyst for a new era of economic growth.

Although my own views on the impact of new technology on the prospects for job creation are closer to those of Schumpeter than of Leontief, it is apparent that the problem of high unemployment will present a formidable challenge for policymakers in both Europe and the United States during the remainder of the 1980s. The responses to this challenge pose considerable political risks to relations among advanced nations in an increasingly interdependent world. These relations are, of course, conditioned not only by the severity of the challenge but also by differing perceptions of the problem, its causes and its proposed cures, on the two sides of the Atlantic. These disparities, in turn, are grounded in differing experiences with employment growth in Europe and the United States over the past decade, as well as in differences in analytical predispositions and in the structure of economic and political institutions in the two regions. Suggestions for alleviating the burdens of high unemployment must be judged not only in terms of their economic efficacy, but also in terms of their implications for the broader relationships between European nations and the United States.

Economic Interdependence and Political Risks

Over the longer term, domestic and international economic objectives are essentially complementary. The performance of the major industrial economies since World War II clearly demonstrates that a rising tide lifts all boats—the enhanced specialization, efficiency and competition associated with rapid growth of trade and investment have stimulated the global economy as well as individual national economies. All too frequently, however, short-term political and economic expediency prevails over longer term considerations. The dangers associated with massive doses of "beggar-thy-neighbor" policies, such as occurred in the 1930s, are widely perceived. But, in an environment of slow growth and high unemployment, political pressures to try to reap short-term benefits from specific encroachments on the rules of open international economic intercourse increase. The danger with such encroachments is that, in the aggregate, they can be significant, particularly if they prompt reciprocal actions.

While continuing high unemployment in Europe and the United States heightens the risk of economic nationalism, the increasing interdependence of the global economy adds significantly to the cost of shortsighted policies. The dramatic expansion of international trade and investment during the postwar period has been a major source of growth and employment opportunities. But it has, in turn, reduced the leeway for individual nations to pursue domestic economic objectives independently of one another. Nor has the system of managed flexibility of exchange rates in effect during the past decade delivered the widely anticipated benefit of greater autonomy of domestic economic policy. And, as international trade and investment have expanded, economic fluctuations among the participating countries appear to have become more and more synchronized.

During the past decade, international economic exposure has grown substantially, and proportionally the greatest increases have taken place in those countries that were previously least exposed. In OECD (Organization for Economic Cooperation and Development) countries, excluding the United States, exports have risen from a 20 percent share of gross domestic product (GDP) in 1970 to 26 percent in 1980. And for the United States, exports of goods and services nearly doubled their share of GDP over the same time frame, rising from 7 percent to 13 percent.

Increasing international investment is another source of growing interdependence. U.S. direct investment abroad, for example, jumped from $76 billion at year-end 1970 to $216 billion in 1980, while foreign ownership of such assets in the United States rose from $13 billion to $68 billion. If one were to include portfolio investments such as securities and bank deposits, U.S. investment abroad totaled $607 billion at the end of 1980 and foreign ownership of U.S. assets totaled $485 billion. These massive investments, and the attendant flows of funds into and out of the United States, illustrate the fact that substantial international influences have been injected into the capital markets, as well as the industrial bases, of many of the major countries of the world.

The emergence of the Organization of Petroleum Exporting Countries, the explosion of inflation during the 1970s, and the two major recessions since the first oil shock further underscore the significant linkage among the world's major industrial economies. In contrast to traditional Keynesian income-expenditure analysis, into which "foreign repercussions" are introduced as second-order effects that alter the magnitude but not the direction of the U.S. economy, the foreign sector may increasingly be generating first-order effects. In fact, during the 1981-82 recession in the United States—the country that was traditionally considered to be least affected by external disturbances—a disproportionate share of the overall weakness was concentrated in the foreign trade sector. The decline in U.S. net exports was equivalent to two-thirds of the falloff in gross national product (GNP) from the middle of 1981, when the economy plunged into the latest recession, to the final quarter of 1982, when a cyclical trough was reached.

Economic policymakers are becoming increasingly aware that they cannot enjoy the best of both worlds. The potential for increased investment, income and employment associated with an open economy cannot harmoniously coexist with the closed-economy freedom to set domestic economic policies without regard to their international implications. Before 1973 it was widely presumed that a move from pegged to flexible exchange rates would enable international economic adjustments to take place automatically, through currency appreciations and depreciations, and would greatly increase national autonomy in the conduct of domestic economic policy. But neither expectation has turned out to be correct.

The experience of the past decade has made it clear that, rather than providing insulation against external disturbances and enhancing the autonomy of domestic macroeconomic policy, the move from pegged rates to managed flexibility has simply transformed the mechanisms and pathways by which disturbances are transmitted internationally. Under pegged rates, for example, the effects of divergent macroeconomic policies were transmitted indirectly through the balance of payments and changes in official holdings of international reserves. This mechanism weakened control of the domestic money stock—a key instrument in managing the level of aggregate demand and the principal policy lever directed toward price stability.

Under the present system, in contrast, external disturbances or divergent policies directly affect relative prices, costs, competitiveness and the balance on current account. In effect, external constraints have resurfaced in the form of a steepened "Phillips curve" (i.e., a worsened short-run trade-off between inflation and unemployment) caused by feedbacks from exchange-rate depreciations to domestic price levels or inflation rates. This situation is often referred to in the economic literature as the problem of vicious and virtuous circles, of inflation-depreciation-inflation in some countries and deflation-appreciation-deflation in others. The political and economic sensitivity of this process, together with the increasing role of the foreign sector in most countries, seems to have made domestic economies more rather than less vulnerable to disturbances originating abroad. Certainly it has made decision-makers in both the public and private sectors increasingly sensitive to excessive movements of both nominal and real (i.e., inflation-adjusted) exchange rates.

The idealized world in which flexible exchange rates enable a nation to adjust payments imbalances relatively effortlessly and in which unemployment is neither exported nor imported has not emerged. Exchange-rate relationships and the resulting interdependence among monetary policies are, in fact, currently a source of tension between the United States and many of its major trading partners. European nations have a sense of being affected and limited by U.S. macroeconomic policies. This perception reflects both the large size of the U.S. economy and the unique position of the U.S. dollar in the international monetary system. The dollar's pivotal position is partly a legacy of its reserve-currency status under the Bretton Woods system, but is due also to the fact that all other major industrialized countries (with the possible exception of Great Britain) regulate their capital markets in ways that effectively restrict the international role their currencies can play.

Europeans are making clear their sense that setting policy in an environment heavily influenced by U.S. economic policies is at times like "sharing a bed with a rogue elephant." There is considerable dissatisfaction overseas with the current mix of relatively tight monetary and stimulative fiscal policies in the United States. The U.S. policy mix is providing an unusually strong dollar and a rebounding U.S. economy—the classic prescription for stimulating the exports of our trading partners. But most European central banks have felt compelled to respond in kind to U.S. monetary policies in order to hold down outflows of capital needed for sustained domestic expansion and minimize the inflationary effects of depreciating currencies. This monetary restraint is, in turn, viewed as a major factor in the sluggishness of economic recovery in Europe. But fiscal restraint also plays an important role. The December 1983 OECD *Economic Outlook* notes, for example, that in contrast with the expansionary budgetary stance of the United States, fiscal policies remain restrictive throughout much of Europe.[3]

With a strong dollar and continuing sluggishness abroad restraining U.S. exports, the United States is experiencing unprecedented deficits in merchandise trade as well as on the more comprehensive current account basis. Both the inflows of capital into the United States from abroad to finance the current-account shortfall and the protectionist pressures that are building in U.S. industries heavily exposed to international competition are sources of political strain on all sides.

Increased capital mobility and the close relationship between interest rates and exchange rates have created an uncomfortable link between developments in financial markets and changes in international competitiveness. Volatility in financial markets has produced volatility in international trade. Concomitantly, in the sphere of public policy, divergences in national monetary policies, and in the mix of monetary and fiscal policies, influence real exchange rates and competitive positions, thus altering the pressures

---

[3] *Economic Outlook*, Paris: Organization for Economic Cooperation and Development, December 1983.

for industrial and trade policies. Persistent overvaluation, for example, can lead to increased pressure for subsidies or import protection, while persistent undervaluation can artificially encourage export activities and reduce the impact of import competition on domestic producers. Conversely, changes in industrial and trade policies alter the pressures on financial variables and monetary policy and contribute to the volatility of exchange rates.[4]

Greater credibility and predictability of policy on both the monetary and the "real" side, together with increased international policy coordination, at least in the restricted sense that each of the leading industrialized nations take into account the exchange-rate effects in determining the "mix" of domestic monetary and fiscal policies, could help to reduce the volatility of real exchange-rate movements around long-term trend values. This damping, in turn, would minimize the misallocation of resources, the pressures for artificial trade restrictions or stimuli, and the potential for political frictions over the international effects of domestic economic policies.

Differing Experiences in the United States and Europe

The marked differences between the American and the European experience during the past decade as regards trends in both unemployment and job creation are likely to influence significantly their policy responses in the future. Although the unemployment rate in the United States during the past ten years has generally been higher than in the major European countries, the rate has risen and fallen cyclically on this side of the Atlantic. In contrast, the European pattern of unemployment has been asymmetric over the business cycle—rising during recessions and tending to level off rather than decline during expansions. As shown in Chart I, the unemployment rate rose rapidly in both regions after the first oil shock. But it came down just as rapidly in the United States once recovery began, while it remained close to its recession peaks throughout most of Europe.

---

[4] J. David Richardson, "The New Nexus Among Trade, Industrial and Exchange-Rate Policies," National Bureau of Economic Research Working Paper, No. 1099, March 1983.

It is still too early to assess the impact of the emerging recovery on unemployment. Although the U.S. unemployment rate is still at historically high levels, it declined rapidly and significantly during 1983—the first year of recovery. In fact, in terms of both employment increases and reductions in the unemployment rate, the first year of recovery in the United States compares quite favorably with past cyclical upturns. The major industrial economies in Europe are, however, trailing behind the American recovery. And there is considerable concern that the slow pace of the European recovery will lead, at best, to only a modest reduction in unemployment. The economies of West Germany and the United Kingdom are currently beginning to turn up but, with policies in France and Italy still focused primarily on inflation and balance-of-payments deficits, a vigorous recovery in Europe seems unlikely, at least in 1984.

The contrast between Europe and the United States in job creation is even more pronounced than in the cyclical behavior of unemployment rates. Employment has risen sharply in the United

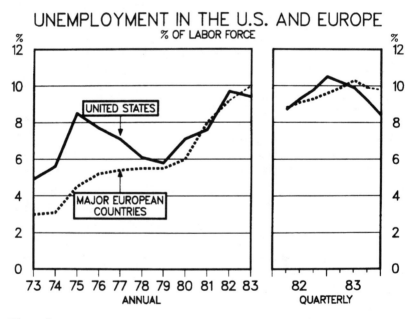

UNEMPLOYMENT IN THE U.S. AND EUROPE

% OF LABOR FORCE

UNITED STATES

MAJOR EUROPEAN COUNTRIES

73 74 75 76 77 78 79 80 81 82 83
ANNUAL

82 83
QUARTERLY

Chart I

States since 1973, while in the major European countries it has actually declined (see Chart II). And even between 1979 and 1983, the average level of U.S. employment was up about two million, or two percent, while it was down slightly in Europe. Much of the employment increase in the United States was concentrated in the service sector. In fact, the United States economy was able to respond to the rapid labor-force expansion engendered by the postwar baby boom and the sharp rise in the participation rates of women during the past decade largely because of the rapid expansion of service-sector employment.

Moreover, the large concentration of women and minorities in the service sector provided some, albeit inadequate, protection against displacement for these groups during the last recession. In the United States, for the first time at a recessionary trough, unemployment rates were higher for men than for women. And even though the chronically high unemployment rates for minorities rose even higher, the largest proportional increases in unemployment were among white males. This pattern may reflect the latter group's relatively high employment in heavy manufacturing—the

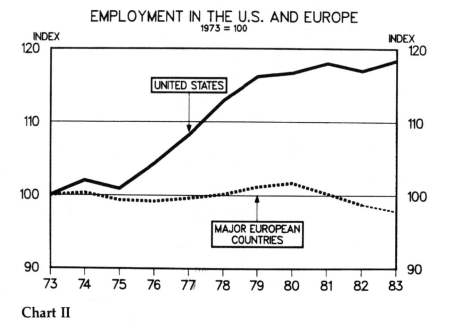

EMPLOYMENT IN THE U.S. AND EUROPE
1973 = 100

Chart II

sector most vulnerable to the energy shocks and the attendant policy responses.

The better record of job creation in the United States appears to be one of the factors holding the average duration of unemployment here well below that in Europe. In the United States during the recent recession, the average duration of unemployment was about four months, compared with seven to ten months for most European countries. Long-term unemployment levels are also much lower on this side of the Atlantic. In several European countries, those jobless for more than a year account for 30 percent or more of the total unemployment—more than double the current proportion in the United States. These divergent experiences in getting the unemployed back to work appear to influence the different explanations of and prescriptions for persistent unemployment in the United States and in the major European countries.

Explanations of Structural Unemployment

Cyclical factors provide, at best, a partial explanation of the divergent trends in unemployment and job creation over the past decade. The recovery in the mid-1970s, following the first oil shock, was much stronger in the United States than in Europe. While the former experienced three years of real GNP growth in the five-percent range after 1975, Europe enjoyed such growth only in 1976, after which it fell back to the range of two to three percent. In contrast, the protracted period of recession and stagnation that has characterized worldwide economic performance since 1979 has been instrumental in pushing unemployment to postwar highs throughout much of the industrialized world. But with unemployment throughout most of Europe on an upward trend even before the latest recession began, and with the "natural" rate of unemployment (i.e., the rate at which further reductions would lead to increased inflationary pressures) in the United States estimated at six to seven percent, explanations of the unemployment problem are increasingly focusing on the structural characteristics and functioning of economies and their constituent markets.

One source of structural imbalance frequently cited by both American and European observers is a faster rise in real wages than in productivity. The explanation of high unemployment derived from classical economics is that one or another of the factors of production has "priced itself out of the market" by increasing its real compensation more rapidly than its rate of productivity increase would allow. The unexpected decline in productivity growth rates throughout the industrialized world, following the first oil shock, apparently combined with inertial elements in the wage-setting process to produce just such a pattern in important sectors in a number of countries.

In the United States, for example, the assumption of three-percent productivity growth is embedded in many labor agreements, making it difficult for wages to adjust fully to a drop in productivity growth. Real compensation, in fact, increased at an average annual rate of 1.3 percent—considerably faster than the 0.8 percent average annual rate of increase in productivity in the United States during the 1970s.

Concerns about the employment effects of high levels of real wages seem to be even more pronounced in Europe. A study recently published by the Brookings Institution shows that real wages rose faster than warranted by productivity growth in the United States and Europe during the 1970s. This study does indicate, however, that the gap between increases in real wages and the productivity growth trend was smaller in the United States than in major European countries such as West Germany and the United Kingdom.[5] In fact, observers on both sides of the Atlantic have recently expressed their concern with the high real wages in Europe. Martin Feldstein, the present Chairman of the U.S. Council of Economic Advisers, recently noted that:

> Real wages in Europe did not adjust adequately to the higher prices of energy and other raw material imports. With real wages too high, firms could not afford to hire enough employees to keep the unemployment rate from rising year after year. . . . This explanation oversimplifies . . . but I believe that it correctly portrays the prime reason for Europe's sustained employment problem.[6]

---

[5] Jeffrey Sachs, "Real Wages and Unemployment in the OECD Countries," *Brookings Papers on Economic Activity*, No. 1, Washington, D.C.: Brookings Institution, 1983.
[6] Martin Feldstein, "Some European Lessons for America's Economic Future," Keynote Address at Rice University, Houston, Texas, February 22, 1983.

Similarly, Otto Lambsdorff, West German Minister of Economics, has argued that "Our economies are still carrying the burden of an excessive real wage level from the seventies. A considerable part of current unemployment is due to the fact that labor has now become too expensive."[7]

Feldstein and other observers have also suggested that liberal social benefits are another important factor underlying Europe's rising structural unemployment. They contend that the combination of extensive unemployment insurance, high health benefits, generous family allowances, and burdensome income tax rates appears to be narrowing the difference between standards of living for those who work and those who do not, to the extent of creating significant disincentives to seeking employment.

Another variant of this "excessive cost" diagnosis focuses on the loss of international wage-price competitiveness because of inappropriate exchange-rate relationships. This point is hardly a new one; one of the main concerns underlying the establishment of the postwar international monetary system and the International Monetary Fund was to forestall a revival of the competitive devaluations that had exacerbated the worldwide depression of the 1930s. But after more than a decade of floating exchange rates, prolonged deviations of the rates between major currencies from values that appear appropriate in terms of underlying economic factors have produced renewed concern about this question. Discussions of these issues over the past two years have focused on the overvaluation of the dollar vis-à-vis the Japanese yen (although the yen and the dollar rose together vis-à-vis most major European countries during 1983) and on the apparently excessive "competitive" devaluations of several smaller European countries.

An alternative view—and a particularly ominous one—of the problem of declining international competitiveness and its associated difficulties downplays the flexible pricing of labor and capital or the competitive pricing of output. It stresses instead the secular decline of certain key manufacturing industries as the root cause of high unemployment levels. In this view, if output in these in-

---

[7] Rudiger Dornbusch, et al., "Macroeconomic Prospects and Policies for the European Community," CEPS Papers, No. 1, Brussels: Centre for European Policy Studies, April 1983.

dustries could somehow be restored to levels closer to existing capacity, displaced workers could be reabsorbed. The so-called Cambridge School of economists has generalized this thesis to entire nations. In their view, Europe has a severe competitive disadvantage in manufacturing that stems from a virtually insurmountable lead possessed by the United States and Japan in technological advances and modernization of the capital stock. And, they contend, this competitive problem can only be addressed behind a shield of generalized trade protection.

Although several of the troubled industries in both Europe and the United States do in fact appear to have cost structures significantly higher than those of their competitors elsewhere, many observers regard low mobility of labor and capital as a more significant factor underlying the persistence of high unemployment. One recent study, for example, concluded that much of the rise in the U.S. unemployment rate for prime-age (25-54) males from 3.1 percent in 1972 to 5.5 percent in 1981 reflects the fact that employment grew in an uneven pattern across geographic areas.[8] European explanations have tended to stress institutional and geographic impediments that are much less important in the United States. Although the legal and institutional barriers to the intercountry movement of labor and capital have diminished somewhat since the European Economic Community was formed, language and cultural factors still make it more difficult for a worker to move his job and his family from Birmingham to Toulouse than from Detroit to Los Angeles.

The most important basis of difference among regions in the degree of factor mobility, however, appears to lie in differences in industrial history and composition. Any advanced industrialized economy is, of course, subject to conflicting pressures: those that tend to increase rigidities by protecting established privileges, such as high wages, worker seniority, etc., and those that tend to loosen them, such as government incentives to mobility. And one of the most effective solvents for built-up rigidities appears to be the growth of new industries, such as electronics, that are unhampered by large sunk costs in existing facilities or by accumulated restric-

---

[8] James L. Medoff, "Labor Markets in Balance," National Bureau of Economic Research, February 1983.

tions on movement and work practices. Long-established industries, like steel, on the other hand, are inevitably less flexible and more resistant to mobility and adaptation.

A higher concentration of long-established industries in some European countries may have resulted, in fact, in a larger accumulation of disincentives to factor mobility and correspondingly greater difficulty in establishing new industries than in the United States—or, even more, in Japan. These differences are not entirely a matter of history. Public policies in Europe appear to be more oriented toward protecting existing jobs than those in the United States. As a result, "exit costs" are generally higher in Europe than in the United States—that is, it is more cumbersome and costly to lay off workers or to relocate or close plants.

An industrial base need not be forever immutable, however, as is demonstrated by developments in regional employment patterns in the United States. New England, for example, has made considerable progress in filling the void left by declining employment in the textile industry with growth in "high tech" areas. And a dynamic business environment appears to underlie the rapid growth of jobs in the southwestern United States. "Booming" Houston and Dallas actually lose a greater proportion of their existing jobs each year than do "stagnating" New Haven or Buffalo. In the two rapidly growing western cities, however, the number of new employment opportunities created annually is significantly in excess of the number of jobs that are phased out.

One of the more interesting developments in recent years has been the institutional changes taking place within the private sector in order to overcome factor immobility and cost inflexibilities. For example, just as the United States is seeing joint ventures between American and Japanese companies that generate new types of labor agreements, so Europe is seeing corporate cross-border acquisitions with government blessing as well as Community-wide employment transfers and placements within particular companies.

That problems of declining industries, loss of competitiveness and factor immobility have indeed added to the burden of unemployment over the past decade is undeniable. What is less clear is the extent to which these difficulties reflect inherent characteristics of an economy rather than the policies and practices of government, labor and industry. There is evidence, for example, that in some European countries, minimum wages, which have risen to a level as high as 70 percent of the median wage, "seriously affected employment prospects for low productivity workers and new labor force entrants."[9] A change in the policies affecting foreign workers may also have contributed to rising unemployment in Western Europe. Since 1973, the countries of the European Economic Community have banned non-EEC labor recruitment. As a result, net emigration has fallen significantly since foreigners in Western Europe are reluctant to leave even during periods of unemployment.

On both sides of the Atlantic, explanations of the unemployment problem have moved beyond an exclusive focus on the level of aggregate demand to concern with the structural functioning and characteristics of economies and their constituent markets. In this latter category, the concerns expressed in both regions have much in common. But there also appear to be important differences in emphasis. Europeans have traditionally tended to accept as given what they regard as more or less permanent structural rigidities, particularly those limiting the mobility of labor and capital, and to shape their economic prescriptions within that framework. At the same time, the OECD Secretariat in its December 1983 *Economic Outlook*, for example, stressed the urgency to European governments of making their economies more flexible and market oriented. In the United States, advocacy of various forms of government-sponsored industrial policy to increase employment opportunities has recently been the focus of increased public attention. Yet, on the whole, American proposals for alleviating structural unemployment tend to focus on increasing the effective functioning of market mechanisms, combined with government-assisted investment in human capital in the form of education and training and the provision of an adequate social "safety net" for those particularly hard hit by the adjustment process.

---

[9] Robert H. Haveman, "Unemployment in Western Europe and the United States: A Problem of Demand, Structure or Measurement?" *American Economic Review*, May 1978.

Cyclical Prescriptions And Trans-Atlantic Frictions

Although there is a wide range of opinion in both Europe and the United States regarding the relative importance of cyclical and structural factors in the persistence of high unemployment, there is also general agreement that a significant part of the problem, particularly the universally sharp rise in unemployment since 1979, is cyclical in origin. Economic growth alone cannot solve all of our employment problems. But economic expansion could, at a minimum, reverse much of the sharp rise in unemployment during the past four years. In fact, the strong recovery in the United States lowered the civilian unemployment rate from nearly 11 percent in December 1982 to slightly above 8 percent at the end of 1983.

Growth is also the best solvent for structural rigidities. And it would be the most effective means to help fund programs that address specific structural problems, such as youth unemployment. Economic expansion would also provide an environment in which real wage gains in excess of productivity growth and/or social benefits that are providing significant disincentives to employment could be pared back with the least social disruption. Moreover, a sustained cyclical recovery would help to diffuse some of the employment-related sources of international friction, such as protectionist pressures.

Unquestionably, a sustainable worldwide recovery would be the most effective short-term antidote to high unemployment and it would facilitate longer term solutions as well. Expansion is well underway in North America. But the United States has not so far performed the locomotive role in launching an export-led recovery throughout Europe. In fact, the current U.S. mix of macroeconomic policies—a relatively tight monetary policy to restrain inflation and a stimulative fiscal stance arising from persistent, large federal government deficits—is a significant source of conflict between Europe and the United States. Many Europeans believe that the high interest rates and overvalued dollar associated with the U.S. policy mix are causing difficulties for them by raising the cost of their imports (including petroleum) whose prices are denominated in dollars. The effect is to increase their domestic inflationary pressures, while high U.S. interest rates drain needed investment funds from Europe. They feel forced to hold their own interest rates above domestically desirable levels in order to stem the outflow of funds and the decline of their currencies, depressing their local economies in the process. The European view appears to be, in other words, that the negative consequences of high interest rates on this side of the Atlantic have more than offset the competitive advantages created by a strong dollar, perhaps reflecting the fact that the United States is a more important factor in the financial markets of the major European economies than in their goods markets.

A better balance between U.S. fiscal and monetary policy would allay some of these frictions. But, as the OECD Secretariat notes in its December 1983 *Economic Outlook*: Europeans "should beware of the proposition that a reduction in U.S. interest rates brought about by fiscal restraint, would by itself improve the prospects for Europe." Dollar depreciation would make the United States more competitive and push up inflation in the United States, leaving less leeway for growth within given monetary targets.[10]

Most of the larger European nations, as well as Japan, maintained the discretionary portions of their government budgets in a restrictive mode during 1982 and 1983, despite the recession. And the December 1983 *Economic Outlook* also notes that the OECD countries as a group, excluding the United States, are expected to experience a substantial further swing toward fiscal restraint in 1984, a development that would impede economic recovery. The OECD Secretariat, as well as a number of other observers, have for some time been contending that those major industrialized nations outside North America where inflation has been significantly reduced could lessen their reliance on export-led expansion and aid global recovery by moving in the direction of greater fiscal stimulus, particularly toward measures focused on stimulating domestic investment. Coordination of such programs of fiscal expansion on a Community-wide basis, they add, could maximize their effectiveness and minimize the associated risks.[11]

U.S. policy regarding exchange-rate intervention is another source of friction between the United States and some major Euro-

---

[10] *Economic Outlook, op. cit..*
[11] Dornbusch, *op. cit..*

pean governments. Many Europeans see the American stand against currency intervention—the flexible-rate version of "benign neglect"—as stemming from the ideological arrogance of a relatively closed economy, which also prints the leading world currency, rather than from genuine skepticism about its effectiveness. This is so despite a recent study by representatives of the major OECD countries that concluded that exchange-market intervention, even if coordinated among countries, was generally ineffective beyond the very short run unless it was accompanied by supporting changes in macroeconomic policies.

Some observers have suggested that the United States might adopt a less doctrinaire stance against intervention in return for a move on the part of the major European nations toward less restrictive trade policies.[12] Over the longer term, a further loosening of some of the restrictive measures that still affect capital markets in most of the major European countries and Japan would allow such currencies as the deutsche mark and the yen to play a larger international role and could facilitate the emergence of more appropriate relationships between these currencies and the dollar.

A sustained recovery on both sides of the Atlantic would, of course, be the most powerful antidote for many of the sources of economic friction currently preoccupying policymakers. The strong U.S. recovery has significantly reduced overall unemployment in North America. But unemployment is still high, particularly in regions such as the Midwest, where many of the industries beset by increasing global competition are concentrated. And recovery has not yet had any noticeable impact on unemployment in Europe. Several northern European nations are in the early stages of recovery; but it is still modest and has not yet spread to some major countries, including France, Italy and Spain.

Elsewhere, the possibility of financial catastrophe arising from the mounting debt problems of many less-developed countries has been averted by the U.S. recovery and a decline in interest rates on dollar-denominated debt, together with a variety of cooperative arrangements among public and private financial institutions and strenuous adjustment measures taken by the debtor countries themselves. But sustained worldwide recovery, along with the

---

[12] Richardson, *op. cit.*.

maintenance of an open world trade environment, represents the only real hope for a durable solution to this still-critical problem.[13]

Prescriptions for Reducing Structural Unemployment

Even if cyclical recovery becomes more widespread and is sustained, unemployment would still pose a significant problem for national policymakers. In the late 1970s, even before the global economy entered a protracted period of recession and economic stagnation, unemployment rates in both the United States and many European countries were significantly above historical norms for the postwar period. A cyclical rebound, particularly one in which the leeway for demand stimulus will be constrained by concerns about renewed inflation, would still leave a substantial problem of structural unemployment in most of the countries with which we are concerned. As with macroeconomic policies for reducing cyclical unemployment, prescriptions for reducing structural unemployment, particularly those that rest on industrial or trade policies, are likely to have significant international consequences. But, in contrast with macroeconomic prescriptions, which by their very nature are systemic, structural remedies must be carefully tailored to the political, social and economic environment and institutions of specific countries.

The more rapid growth rate of real wages than of productivity underlies at least some of the structural unemployment problem. However, there has been a significant deceleration in real wage growth in the United States and Europe since the start of the 1980 recession. In the United States considerable attention has been focused during the past two years on the possibilities of reducing wage scales in some industries with particularly high levels of unemployment and excess capacity, financial difficulties, and com-

---

[13] William R. Cline, *International Debt and the Stability of the World Economy*, Washington, D.C.: Institute for International Economics, 1983. The results of Cline's comprehensive study of this issue, for example, "strongly suggest at least 2.5 percent [OECD] growth must be achieved in 1984-86 in order for the debt problem to improve. With growth of 3 percent . . . there is a sufficiently clear trend of declining relative size of deficits and debt that the situation [less-developed countries' debt problems] remains manageable. . . . At higher growth (3.5 percent) the improvement is even sharper."

petitive pressures. Actual wage reductions, or at least postpone-
ment or elimination of scheduled increases have, in fact, been
accepted by workers in the airline, trucking, auto, steel and several
smaller industries as part of a comprehensive effort to restore the
competitive viability of particular firms or entire industries.

Such selective adjustments are more difficult to make in Europe
where wage negotiations tend to be more centralized. Although
periodic recommendations for generalized national wage freezes
have not been implemented anywhere, a number of developments
have slowed wage growth. The wage increases negotiated during
the last two years in West Germany and Great Britain have fallen
relative to both actual and anticipated rates of inflation, implying a
moderation in real wage growth. And in other countries, such as
Italy, Belgium and the Netherlands, cost of living formulas are
being pared down. Increases in minimum wages and in the salaries
of government workers were also curtailed in the Netherlands,
while in France price controls and moral suasion appear to be
having some restraining effect on wage increases.

Increased flexibility of compensation is an alternative or, perhaps, a complement to more moderate rates of wage increase in
conventional labor agreements. A less rigid wage-setting system
would lessen the need for employment to serve as the "slack vari-
able" that absorbs a large proportion of the shocks created by
changes in demand. The potential for inflationary wage settlements might also be reduced with greater flexibility of compensation in the form of an increased role for profit sharing in total
remuneration. Henry Wallich, a governor of the Federal Reserve
Board, has suggested, "taking a leaf of the wisdom of Japan,"
where a significant proportion of annual pay in large firms comes
from profit-related bonuses. Wallich argues that, with a bonus in
prospect, the front-loaded component of wage settlements could
be significantly reduced.[14]

Another category of prescriptions for relieving unemployment
involves altering the functioning of labor markets. Some economists have suggested that selective employment subsidies may enable policymakers "to cheat the Phillips curve"—that is to stimu-

---

[14] Leonard Silk, "Recovery from the Era of Shocks," *The New York Times*, January 8, 1984, III, p. 1.

late rapid growth in employment without igniting inflationary pressures.[15] Employment subsidies are, in fact, widely used. Opinions vary as to their effectiveness, but there is widespread agreement that they are most likely to be effective if they are marginal rather than general and are targeted at groups in substantial excess supply, such as teenagers, so as to increase their employment opportunities without placing significant upward pressure on wages. Wage subsidies are generally designed to increase demand for particular groups of labor or in particular geographical areas, while non-wage subsidies are typically directed toward increasing the effective supply of labor. Non-wage subsidies include government-assisted worker training, improved information on job opportunities over broad geographical areas, and assistance in meeting relocation expenses.

Job sharing represents yet another approach to alleviating the pain caused by substantial unemployment. Under such programs the length of the workweek is reduced or two workers share one full-time job. The idea is to lessen the hardship of a given level of unemployment by spreading it around, on the assumption that the hardship of two underemployed workers is less than that of one worker with no job at all. While this point is not itself susceptible to economic evaluation, proposals for implementing the job-sharing concept do in fact raise some economic issues.

Although job sharing need not in principle affect economic efficiency, its actual implementation is likely to have such effects. On the positive side is the possibility that, at least in some cases, greater flexibility of the work schedule may reduce absenteeism and enhance the vigor of workers on the job. And job sharing by young people may enhance their long-term employability by giving work experience to larger numbers. On the negative side are the increased managerial burden and the increase in the non-wage portion of unit labor costs that occurs because employment taxes and such benefits as medical care tend to be proportional to the number of employees rather than to the number of hours worked.

---

[15] Martin N. Baily and James Tobin, "Macroeconomic Effects of Selective Public Employment and Wage Subsidies," *Brookings Papers on Economic Activity*, No. 2, 1977.

In practice, the job sharing concept frequently involves a call for reduced working hours with no accompanying reduction in total wages. Such proposals, obviously, entail a substantial increase in labor costs. In addition to increasing inflationary pressures and reducing competitiveness in the nation introducing them, such measures represent subsidies to inefficient employment borne directly by the affected employers.

Industrial and trade policies are, increasingly, high on the list of options under consideration as palliatives for structural unemployment. Indeed, old-fashioned trade policies are more and more becoming intertwined with and enmeshed in domestic industrial policies aimed at directing resources toward industries that either appear to have high growth potential or are experiencing what are believed to be temporary difficulties. Industrial policy frequently involves sector or industry-specific government support either in the form of some type of subsidy (including tax advantages or capital allocations or guaranties) or protection against competitive pressures, or some combination of the two.

The rationales for such measures fall into several main categories: the future promise of an "infant" industry, the preservation or restoration of a substantial number of jobs, or the significance of particular industries to national security, defined in either military or economic terms. Because industries with uncompetitive cost structures often cannot generate the investment funds necessary to make them competitively viable, public or publicly guaranteed investment or trade protection is frequently urged to assist their modernization. Such concerns underlie the demands for voluntary restraint covering the export of Japanese automobiles to the United States and a number of other countries, and of video equipment to Europe. A further rationale for protection is as a cushion to reduce the personal, social and political costs associated with the labor displacement caused by rapid shifts in global competitive patterns, particularly during periods of slow growth and high unemployment.

While disagreements over measures that restrict trade are perennial, there has been increasing concern recently, particularly in the United States, with the trade distortions created by government subsidies provided in a variety of forms to a number of important European industries. Since the United States is not without trade-related subsidies of its own, such as the Domestic International Sales Corporation—which permits an indefinite deferral of direct taxes on income earned from exports from the United States—some Europeans view the U.S. criticism as hypocritical.

The most severe problems of trade and employment coalesce in industries, such as steel, where some countries are attempting to reduce production in the face of worldwide excess capacity while at the same time other countries, principally in the developing world, are expanding productive capacity as part of their development programs.

The Europeans argue that their subsidies to steel production are domestic subsidies that are not designed to increase exports and, as such, are allowable under the General Agreement on Tariffs and Trade (GATT). But the U.S. steel industry, which is also confronted with severe problems of unemployment and overcapacity, contends that the European subsidies have an injurious effect on its business and therefore constitute a legitimate basis for compensatory protection. A number of countervailing measures have in fact been instituted in the United States in recent years, and others are currently being proposed. The EEC, which has recently strengthened cartel-like controls on steel production and prices, resents the increasingly restricted access to the U.S. market, which it regards as a legitimate "safety valve" in its efforts to restructure the European steel industry.

Irrespective of the merits of the arguments advanced by the antagonists in this debate, the "steel controversy" between the United States and Europe indicates clearly how completely intermingled industrial and trade policies—or at least trade effects—can become. Moreover, the frictions originating with steel are spreading to other sectors. In January 1984 the EEC notified the GATT of its intention to impose retaliatory quotas and tariff increases on U.S. exports of selected sporting goods, plastics, chemicals and alarms to compensate for quotas and tariffs placed by the United States on specialty steel items the previous July. Moreover, some observers believe that increased restrictions on agricultural products currently under consideration by the EEC are, in part, motivated by a desire to retaliate for U.S. restrictions on specialty steel imports. The competitiveness of other industries on both sides of the Atlantic is also being affected by these policies. Measures that restrict the availability of products, like steel, which are heavily used in the making of other goods, tend to raise production costs for the latter industries and, in turn, make it more difficult for their domestic manufacturers to compete in the global marketplace. As a result there are often increasing pressures for protection of these industries as well.

Another category of prescriptions for relieving structural unemployment involves a growing list of measures that would not merely take the immobility of labor and capital as a given, but would restrict it further. Among these are the provisions of the EEC's Vredeling proposal that would require advance notification, extensive labor-management consultations and waiting periods before decisions likely to affect the work force—such as plant closings or production shifts—could be implemented. The intent is presumably to minimize the trauma of unanticipated layoffs, to permit individuals and communities to plan for changed circumstances and, perhaps, to allow them to marshal arguments and alternative proposals (as well as political pressures) to forestall a particular decision. Such proposals are also regarded by their proponents as a way of making the workplace more democratic through consultations with workers on key managerial decisions. These types of measures are, however, likely to entail significant economic costs. The imposition of an additional layer of regulatory processes creates costs of delay in implementing decisions. By reducing rather than increasing economic mobility, the natural processes of economic adjustment are lengthened and made more costly, and competitiveness is reduced.

Reducing structural unemployment poses a major challenge to policymakers in Europe and the United States. Its causes, and therefore its cures, are manifold and incompletely understood. Cyclical recovery cannot, by definition, reduce structural unemployment, but it will create an environment more conducive to dealing with the problem. Even then, policymakers will face the dual challenge of increasing the mobility of labor and capital to create both new job opportunities and an increased ability to take advantage of them and, at the same time, of cushioning the hardships of displacement and adjustment for those hardest hit by change. But these essential objectives are in part antithetical: measures that cushion the adjustment process, such as liberal unemployment benefits, may also reduce incentives to adjust. Some measures, like retraining subsidies or relocation assistance, can contribute to both objectives, but some trade-offs are inevitable.

Such trade-offs and, more generally, effective policy prescriptions for reducing structural unemployment, must encompass a variety of economic, political and social objectives and must be tailored to the traditions and institutions of each nation. There are no universal guidelines, for example, on the appropriate level or type of government assistance that should be provided to workers facing displacement from their jobs for technological or competitive reasons. Similarly, appropriate inducements to the creation of jobs for particular groups that are hard to employ will vary from one country to another. But, over the long term, public policies will foster increased employment opportunities and minimize international frictions if their basic thrust is directed toward encouraging investment to upgrade a nation's capital stock and increase the employability of its "human capital"—its citizenry—through enhanced basic education, training or retraining, and functional and geographical mobility.

European and American Perspectives on Current Unemployment Problems

Differences in philosophical perspective and in the patterns of employment and unemployment experienced over the past decade have interacted to shape and differentiate American and European views regarding the causes and cures of high unemployment. While there is a growing belief on both sides of the Atlantic that measures affecting the structure and functioning of markets must supplement macroeconomic manipulation of aggregate demand, there are important differences in the focus and emphasis devoted to various types of microeconomic interventions. In general, it appears that more attention is focused in Europe on policy analyses and proposals that directly affect the structure of employment and job tenure than in the United States. And in the United States there seems to be more emphasis on making markets more flexible and competitive.

One must not oversimplify, of course, nor exaggerate the extent of trans-Atlantic differences. Pessimism regarding the economic future, and an accompanying resistance to change and the economic adjustments it requires, are growing in the United States as well as in Europe. These attitudes foster increasing interest in industrial subsidies, protection, plant-closing legislation and job-sharing schemes that would accept structural rigidities as inevitable and actually increase them while attempting to render more equitable the sharing of the burdens thus created. And there are wide differences in attitude and emphasis within the European nations. West Germany, for example, has traditionally tended more toward what is here characterized as the "American" rather than the "European" view. Indeed, the persistence of such differences in policy prescriptions among the nations of Europe can significantly affect competitive relationships and trade patterns. If, for example, the downward adjustment of wage and price trends proceeds further and faster in West Germany than in other countries belonging to the European Monetary System, this will create a source of persistent pressure for upward revaluation of the deutsche mark within the EMS.

These differences in attitude regarding the causes of high unemployment and policy prescriptions for dealing with it are also bound to affect receptivity toward the automation of manufacturing processes—a development with dramatic potential to reduce costs and drudgery, increase productivity and competitiveness, enhance potential output and income, and at the same time quicken the pace of technological change to which individuals and economic structures must adapt.

A point of universal agreement, of course, is that the current high level of unemployment is unacceptable, from an economic, political, social and moral perspective, in Europe and the United States. But our prescriptions must respond to long-term needs as well as short-term problems; nothing would be gained if the remedial effects were ephemeral. Just as many of the current unemployment problems in the industrialized world are an outgrowth of misguided policies of the past, short-term fixes would only sow the seeds of greater problems in the future.

Having stated the obvious caution, where does this array of competing explanations of and suggested solutions to the unemployment crisis leave us? A sustainable expansion on both sides of the Atlantic is an essential first step for easing the political frictions associated with current unemployment problems and creating an environment in which policymakers can effectively address the more stubborn structural problems. Carefully designed subsidies can help to alleviate structural unemployment. But, in my view, the basic thrust of policy must be directed toward encouraging greater productivity and competitiveness. The link between productivity growth and increased employment opportunities is not always obvious. But, in fact, real incomes can only grow on a sustainable basis if productivity rises. And, historically, rising real incomes have generated the greater demands for goods and services and investment that have provided the increased opportunities for an expanding work force. Contemporary international comparisons reinforce the point: Japan, which since the mid-1960s has had the highest rate of productivity increase among the principal industrialized nations, has also had the lowest average unemployment rate—less than two percent—while the United States and the United Kingdom, whose productivity growth rates have been among the lowest, have experienced unemployment rates considerably above the average of the other industrialized nations.

Leontief is right, of course; the technology of the future is different in important ways from the advances of the past, which largely replaced physical effort. There does not seem to be any intrinsic reason, however, why this latest wave of technological progress should not create new employment opportunities. The historical record, after all, is of technological advances leading to better products, lower prices and increases in productivity, demand, employment and income. It takes a certain act of faith to assume that past patterns will prevail in the future, or even to assert that the sun will indeed rise in the East again tomorrow morning. One can never prove conclusively that things will be the same this time or that catastrophe will not occur. But even though we cannot be certain exactly where future opportunities will arise, it would be foolish to jettison the evidence of the past and take the view that the best we will be able to do in the future is to share an inadequate pool of jobs.

This does not mean that we can afford to wait passively and let the future happen. We must foster an environment that encourages progress, but at the same time we cannot lose sight of the need to help individuals adapt to change. Painful adjustments have accompanied the shift in the employment base from agriculture toward manufacturing and, more recently, toward the increasing relative importance of the heterogeneous category called services. Today, in the midst of a period of rapid and stressful transition, modern standards of equity and emphasis on security place many demands on us to minimize these adjustment costs and to spread them fairly, particularly in terms of creating new employment opportunities for displaced workers. The policy challenge is to ease the pain of transition in ways that encourage rather than retard growth.

Freezing ourselves in time, so to speak, has never been a path to expanding employment opportunities. But in this electronic age, policies aimed at maintaining the status quo would be particularly costly. Such policies would not only sacrifice opportunities for long-term growth but, as the competitive gap widened and pressures mounted, would be increasingly likely to fail even in their immediate objectives. There are no magic potions or alchemists' stones for achieving sustainable increases in productivity and growth and improving competitiveness. However, the current malaise in Europe suggests strongly that measures to enhance competition and promote increased economic integration of European markets are urgently needed, along with policies to enhance profitability, increase private investment, lower the costs of employment, improve the availability of capital to new businesses, and encourage entrepreneurial risk taking. The United States, on the other hand, in the view of the President's Commission on Industrial Competitiveness, needs to improve the educational system and opportunities for its citizens, encourage investment in research and development, strengthen the access of new business to low-cost capital, and lessen administrative impediments to exports.[16] While Europe might profitably take some leaves from America's book with respect to market integration, technological innovation and job creation, the United States might, in turn, scrutinize carefully some of the European efforts at managing people, such as the West German apprenticeship system, for their applicability to American conditions.

---

[16] The Presidential Commission has not released its final report, at this writing. But Rimmer de Vries, a member of the commission, supplied this information in his remarks at an economic symposium in Jackson, Mississippi, January 11, 1984.

The Spillover into Trans-Atlantic Relations

The persistence of high unemployment on both sides of the Atlantic, and the differences in representative American and European views regarding the mix of factors underlying this phenomenon and the policies most likely to alleviate it, have identifiable implications for the state of relations between the United States and its West European allies. The apparent intractability of the unemployment problem, plus a growing sense of the vulnerabilities—as well as the opportunities—created by increased economic interdependence in a world subject to severe economic shocks, has increased pressures for defensive economic nationalism. Such nationalism is defensive in the sense that it is based not on the desire to extend national powers beyond one's own borders, but rather on a desire to regain control over economic developments within one's borders. This is occurring in an environment of increased vulnerability to disturbances originating abroad and expanded governmental responsibility for the fulfillment of a variety of domestic economic objectives, including high employment combined with reasonable price stability.

As we have discussed in some detail here, there are substantial divergences between representative European and American views on how to deal with the unemployment problem. These divergences are rooted in differences in intellectual traditions, as well as in different experiences with trends in employment and unemployment over the past decade or more. This absence of broadly agreed upon solutions is hardly surprising; indeed, it is critically important that policy prescriptions be carefully tailored to the political and economic structures and institutions of the particular country for which they are prescribed. At the same time, it is equally important that such national policies be designed so as to minimize the friction generated where they overlap and impinge on one another.

This caution becomes more and more urgent in the face of developments that are likely to enhance the potential for such friction during the remainder of the decade. On the one hand, as we have noted earlier, demographic and social factors are likely to intensify structural unemployment pressures in Europe by increasing the inflow of new and inexperienced workers into the labor force, while simultaneously reducing them in the United States. At the same time, the widely divergent experiences with job creation on the two continents over the past two decades are being projected into the future by the contrast between the strong U.S. economic recovery and the so-far anemic European one. Finally, Europe is clearly suffering from a growing crisis of confidence as regards its technological dynamism and competitive strength. While North America has focused on its competitive position vis-à-vis Japan, Europeans are convinced of the United States' technological leadership and underlying competitive strength, the latter currently masked, in their view, by an overvalued dollar.

Countless words have been written, by this author along with many others, about the need for greater policy coordination in a world of increased economic interdependence. But the urgency of the situation, and the lack of progress toward such coordination, requires that we be both more specific and perhaps more modest in our demands. In the area of macroeconomic policy, the fact that flexible exchange rates do not and cannot provide insulation against disturbances originating abroad, nor autonomy in the conduct of domestic economic policies, indicates that some degree of what might be called positive coordination is essential. Although the degree of macroeconomic stimulus or restraint governments exercise at any particular time will inevitably be dictated primarily by domestic economic conditions, it is essential that governments take into account to the maximum degree possible the external effects of the particular mix of monetary and fiscal policies through which their overall macroeconomic stance is achieved. This is because, as we have discussed in some detail here, this policy mix has a major impact on a nation's exchange rate, at least in the case of those larger industrialized countries with relatively unfettered financial markets. And, under the current system of managed flexibility, changes in exchange rates are a major vehicle for transmission of economic fluctuations across national boundaries.

The role of the United States in this process is particularly important, since the unique role of the dollar in the international monetary system means that its overvaluation—or undervaluation—relative to other major currencies is likely to exert deflationary—or inflationary—pressure on the global economy as a whole. But the United States cannot carry the burden alone; the European nations and Japan must share the task of keeping exchange-rate relationships in reasonable alignment by paying increased attention to the effects of their fiscal, monetary and financial policies on the external value of their currencies.

A closely related point is the need for nations to try to maintain some rough check on the consistency of their macroeconomic goals with those of their major partner countries, since inconsistency in this respect is likely to produce both mutual frustration and a collective excess of either stimulus or restraint in the global economy. To be more specific, in a world where all countries cannot simultaneously export more than they import, and where it is no longer realistic nor practicable to regard the United States as a "locomotive" capable of pulling the rest of the world along into high employment and noninflationary prosperity, excessive reliance on export-led growth is likely to result in a sort of international game of "hot potato," whereby nations count on the foreign trade sector as the major source of expanded employment opportunities, even if it means increasing the short-term unemployment pressures in other countries. The result of such inconsistencies in expectations and in the policies to which they lead is likely to be widespread frustration with respect to the ultimate impact on employment and, in many cases, rising protectionist pressures.

It is in the area of microeconomic policies aimed at attenuating the structural unemployment that cannot be abolished by economic recovery alone that the prescriptions range most widely and require the most careful tailoring to the economic, political and social characteristics of each country. One cannot make airtight distinctions, of course, as we have noted in this discussion. There is considerable interaction and feedback between monetary and fiscal policies on the one hand and trade and industrial policies on the other. And a country can beggar-its-neighbors equally through policies that limit imports or subsidize exports directly, or that distort the external value of its currency. Nonetheless, with respect to microeconomic policies that affect primarily the structure— rather than the aggregate level—of domestic economic activity, the major need is to avoid international spillover and friction in the form of negative effects imparted through international trade and investment transactions. Otherwise, the United States and its European allies are likely to develop lengthening "bills of particulars" (i.e., lists of complaints about economic behavior across the Atlantic) that are bound to affect political relationships as well.

In some cases, the link between trade issues and foreign policy concerns is direct as, for example, in the case of the gas pipeline issue and other questions relating to East-West trade. Here, the Europeans clearly felt that divergences between their views and those of the United States were grounded not only in differing perceptions of the most appropriate behavior toward the Soviet Union in terms of political and security considerations, but also on the vastly different importance of East-West trade in affecting domestic levels of output and employment in European countries as opposed to the United States. The fact that this issue was ultimately resolved at the highest political levels indicates how grave was the concern that it might otherwise threaten the solidarity of the NATO Alliance.

In the case of more straightforward "old fashioned" trade disputes, the link to concerns about domestic unemployment, particularly its structural component, is even more obvious. We have already noted the trade frictions created by efforts to manage the problems posed for nations on both sides of the Atlantic by the decline of their domestic steel industries. Without delving here into the merits of the case, it is clear that both the subsidies granted by the EEC to steel producers under the Davignon plan and the import restraints that the United States has imposed or may impose in response to those subsidies are responses to fears about the economic, social and political repercussions of declining unemployment in a large traditional manufacturing sector with substantial worldwide overcapacity. And the ripples from a particular trade dispute tend to spread. Many observers feel that the tightening of restraints on imports of American agricultural products currently under consideration by the EEC may be adopted at least partly in retaliation against U.S. restraints on imports of European steel, or at least used as a bargaining chip in negotiations. Whether the resolution of such issues lies in the development of new "rules for intervention" to replace what many regard as the "outmoded" rules of an increasingly bypassed GATT or in the rejuvenation of the GATT framework and its extension to such areas of critical concern as trade in services, high technology products and international investment, some new initiatives are urgently needed.

The impact of policymakers' preoccupation with persistent unemployment in their own countries on the internal functioning of the EEC also has implications for relationships between that body and the United States. Fears about job displacement in current member countries are slowing and making more difficult the further expansion of the EEC by increasing resistance to the entry of Spain and Portugal, countries with a relatively low-wage, underemployed labor force. And the two closely related issues that are currently threatening the very fabric of the EEC—the distribution of the budgetary burden and its implications for agricultural policies—reflect a strong link between domestic economic difficulties and policies affecting external relationships. The issue of budgetary contributions, always a thorny one, is exacerbated by the impact of slow growth and high unemployment on the tax revenues and welfare burdens of the governments of member countries. In an effort to resolve the resulting impasse, the EEC is increasingly seeking ways to hold down the subsidy elements in its wide-ranging programs of support for European agriculture. The most obvious way to hold down subsidies while maintaining the overall degree of support is by tightening restraints on imports of agricultural products and, as we have already noted, that is exactly what appears to be happening. This is but one more instance, albeit a somewhat complex one, of the general proposition that persistent economic difficulties at home tend to make nations more inward looking and protectionist in their economic relations with other countries, and less willing to take into account the needs of the global economy.

In sum, relations between the United States and its allies in Western Europe appear to be affected at the moment by the coincidence of two difficult and painful periods of transition. On the one hand, these advanced industrialized nations are having to adjust to a variety of economic transitions: from inflaton to disinflation; from cheap to expensive energy; and from primarily bilateral to far more generalized global competition in manufactured goods where they are no longer the low-cost producers in many industries. Inevitably, the costs of adjustment involved in these transitions, essential as they are, have been reflected in structural problems in labor markets.

At the same time, relations among these countries are shaped by a still-uncompleted political transition, from a world of undisputed American hegemony in the Western world to one in which there is no longer any hegemonial power. In the past, U.S.-European relations were shaped by an unspoken compact. On the one hand, the United States was frequently willing to subordinate its short-term, narrowly conceived, economic interests to the long-term political and economic advantages of both strengthened economies in other free-world nations and a viable trading and monetary system linking those nations. The European nations, on the other hand, were willing to accord the United States certain special privileges (primarily that of printing international money) as a concomitant of the special responsibilities it undertook for the military security and economic stability of the noncommunist world..

This implicit bargain no longer holds. In the political sphere, the complexity of the "Euromissile" debate suggests considerable fragmentation of political consensus regarding the extent to which the United States should provide, and the Europeans should rely on, an American-held nuclear umbrella. And in the economic sphere, the growing urgency of domestic economic problems has lessened the focus of U.S. policymakers on attending to the needs of the global economy. Europe, in turn, is torn between its desire for a symmetrical system in which the United States behaves and is treated "just like everyone else" and its preoccupation with the significant role still played by the U.S. economy and economic policies in the health of their own economies. Together, the trans-Atlantic partners are trapped in a time warp, between the hegemonial organization of the postwar past and the more collective forms of leadership and responsibility required for the future, but for which neither the conceptual framework nor the implementing institutions have yet been sufficiently developed.

A comprehensive prescription for leading us successfully through this period of multiple transitions is, of course, beyond the scope of this discussion. But some general observations do emerge from this survey of the present landscape. On the European side, there is an urgent need to reestablish momentum toward market integration, technological innovation and a sharpened competitive edge. For only then are the nations of Europe likely to focus more on growth and adjustment to market forces and less on preservation and protection, to emphasize outward-looking rather than inward-looking solutions to their economic difficulties, and to move away from what Gardner Patterson, former Deputy Director General of the GATT, has termed "the EC propensity toward bilateralism and sectoral arrangements . . . [and its] tolerance of, even affection for, discriminatory practices."[17]

For its part, the United States must increasingly take account of the external effects of its domestic economic policies and the means by which they are implemented—a need exemplified by the current concern with the global impact of high real interest rates in the United States. At the same time, it is essential that we restore at home economic and political conditions that could reverse the present buildup of pressures for protection.

If progress is made on these fronts, the foundation may be laid for a renewed "implicit bargain" between Europe and the United States. In such a bargain, the United States might take greater account of the trans-Atlantic spillover of its economic policies and curb its tendency toward "global unilateralism"—efforts to assert extraterritorial jurisdiction and impose universal rules of behavior that have long been a source of irritation to our allies—in return for an increased willingness on the part of the European nations (along with Japan) to share responsibility for maintaining Western security, the viability of the international trade and financial systems, and the health of the global economy.

One final point is worth noting. We have already underscored the fact that, in terms of economic effectiveness, policies stressing economic growth and productivity increases must be central to any program for alleviating high unemployment and enhancing job opportunities and individual economic welfare. But this view is supported by political considerations as well. For it is only in the context of economic growth that nations can hope to find solutions to their domestic unemployment problems without resort to policies that attempt to export these difficulties, thus complicating the problems of other countries and increasing points of friction among them. And it is only if such solutions are found, if the severity of unemployment is substantially alleviated without in-

---

[17] Gardner Patterson, "The European Community as a Threat to the System," in *Trade Policy in the 1980s*, ed. William R. Cline, Cambridge: MIT Press, 1983.

creased resort to beggar-thy-neighbor policies, that the nations of the Atlantic Alliance will be able to forge new and more effective mechanisms for managing relations among themselves and for enhancing their ability to take on greater collective responsibilities for leadership in the Western world.

I acknowledge with thanks the valuable assistance of Edgar J. Sullivan of General Motors Economic Staff in the preparation of this paper.

Raymond Barre

National Versus International Solutions for Unemployment

From the end of World War II until the beginning of the 1970s, West European countries, on the whole, enjoyed full employment. Since the first "oil shock" in 1973, and above all, since the second one in 1979-80, they have experienced a marked increase in unemployment. Currently, joblessness is a phenomenon that seriously affects them all as the result of both cyclical and structural factors. Before the current world economic crisis, Europe benefited from a more favorable situation than the United States. Since 1974 the evolution of unemployment has been roughly similar in the two regions. But this is no longer true now that a recovery has begun and is accelerating in the United States.

Forecasts made by the Organization of Economic Cooperation and Development (OECD) for the period from 1984 to mid-1985 show that the rate of unemployment will remain high in European countries and will even continue to grow. In contrast, it will fall rapidly in the United States, where four million jobs were created during the second half of 1983.

Unemployment is a major economic, social and political problem in West European countries. It raises many questions concerning the economic policies that should be implemented in order to reduce unemployment; the proper coordination of economic policies not only among European Economic Community (EEC) members but also among the other industrialized countries; the effects of U.S. economic policy on the evolution of other economies, specifically by means of interest rates and exchange rates; and international trade problems, especially the development of protectionist tendencies.

In my view the solution of the unemployment problem in European countries has to be found in a vigorous and continuous national effort by each of them to restore price stability and a balance-of-payments equilibrium and to adapt their economies to international competition while avoiding protectionist measures.

To be sure, a better convergence of economic policies among industrialized countries would contribute to a more rapid improvement of economic conditions. Yet this convergence ultimately depends on the political will of each government, and on the pressure of events, more than on international mechanisms for the coordination of economic policies. The "summits" among the industrialized countries, the regular meetings among OECD or EEC ministers, can create better understanding; they have not thus far created effective obligations for governments. Each country is ready to consider the wishes expressed by its partners or by international organizations or to listen to very discreet advice from them. Nonetheless, in practice each country vigilantly safeguards its freedom of action in making economic policy. The United States example is significant in this respect.

Rapid progress toward a genuine international coordination of economic policies is not likely in the foreseeable future (although this objective should be constantly pursued). Therefore, it behooves each country to solve its problems through its own efforts. Above all each nation has to put its house in order, taking account of increasing economic interdependency in the world, averting beggar-thy-neighbor policies, and respecting international commitments.

I. Trends in Employment and Unemployment:
1975 to 1982

Three facts have characterized the evolution of employment in Europe and the United States since 1975 (Table I):

1) The work force continued to grow in Europe during the period under consideration. Nonetheless its growth was much less dynamic than in the United States where the work force grew more rapidly. In addition, U.S. employment rates have been higher than European rates. (The difference is very noticeable for women: 61.5 percent of American working-age women participate in the labor force compared to 48.6 percent in OECD Europe.)

TABLE I

Trends in the Growth of Work Force and of Total Employment
1975 to 1982

	United States		OECD Europe	
	1975-1979	1979-1982	1975-1979	1979-1982
Growth of work force (average annual rate in percent)	2.8	1.6	0.6	0.6
Growth of total employment (average annual rate in percent)	3.5	0.3	0.0	−0.7

	1970	1975	1979	1982	1970	1975	1979	1982
Unemployment rate (% of work force)[1]	4.8	8.3	5.7	9.5	3.3	5.0	5.6	9.3

[1] Corrected Data

Source: Employment Outlook, Organization for Economic Cooperation and Development, September 1983.

Employment rates have increased more rapidly for women and diminished less rapidly for men in the United States relative to Europe during the same period.

2) Total employment stagnated or decreased in Europe while it increased noticeably in the United States. In the United States, even though the period from 1979 to 1982 was marked by two recessions, employment still increased (plus .03 percent annually); in Europe, it decreased (minus .07 percent annually).

3) Unemployment increased in the two regions, but in Europe the situation has grown steadily worse since 1970 while in the United States there have been wide fluctuations.

Between 1975 and 1979, the decline in unemployment in the United States is attributable to the fact that employment grew more rapidly than did the work force. In Europe the increase in unemployment is due to a stagnation in job growth against the background of a slow increase in the work force.

Between 1979 and 1982, the United States and Europe were in similar situations: the difference between the growth of the work force and the growth of total employment is the same for both regions (1.3 percent in the two areas according to the OECD); the growth in unemployment rates was comparable (3.8 percent in the United States and 3.7 percent in Europe); the total percentage of unemployed in Europe and the United States was of the same order (9.5 percent in the United States and 9.3 percent in Europe). As for Europe, the average rate of unemployment varied significantly from country to country. The situation in 1982 was worst in Spain (15.9 percent), in Belgium (13 percent) and in Britain (12.5 percent). France (8 percent) and Italy (8.9 percent) occupied a median position. The Federal Republic of Germany enjoyed the most favorable situation (6 percent), while Sweden (3.1 percent) and Norway (2.4 percent) were special cases.

At first glance, thus, it would seem as if it were possible to explain the relative position of the two regions with regard to unemployment *by the respective increases in the resources of manpower and jobs.* To be sure, these changes are profoundly different in the United States and Europe. But their unemployment rates until 1983 were comparable.

From early 1984 until mid-1985 unemployment will be cause for greater concern in Western Europe than in the United States. A bright recovery in the United States has permitted employment to advance at a rapid pace with a sharp decrease in unemployment. On the contrary, Europe seems likely to suffer increasing unemployment. All the major European nations will be affected—except Britain, which should enjoy stabilization but at a high rate of unemployment, and, perhaps, West Germany, if the present recovery is stronger throughout the rest of 1984 than is now expected (Table II).

TABLE II

Projections of Unemployment

Unemployment rate[1] (% of work force)	1983	1984	1985 (1st quarter)
United States	9.5	8.0	7.75
OECD Europe	10.5	11.25	12.0

[1] National Data

Source: Economic Outlook, OECD, December 1983.

The decade of the 1980s should thus possess two characteristics: —in both Europe and the United States, unemployment will persist at levels two times higher than before the first oil shock; —nonetheless, unlike the situation that prevailed in the 1960s, Europe will be harder hit than North America.

Some Characteristics of *Employment* in the United States and Europe

The *distribution by sectors of jobs* that have been created since 1975 in the United States and Europe has one feature in common in both regions: the importance of *the service sector* in the growth of employment. With respect to industry, however, the difference is considerable: from 1975 to 1981, industry in North America created five million jobs , whereas it eliminated some three million in Europe. This development shows clearly that growth in the service sector does not necessarily take place at the expense of the industrial sector (Table III).

Despite this development, employment in the service sector in the United States accounts for a much more significant part of total employment than in Europe: 68 percent compared to 51 percent.

A comparison of the growth of employment at the various levels of *government* in the United States and Europe is equally very instructive (Table IV).

During the last two decades, but mainly since the beginning of the world economic crisis, the growth of government employment in Europe has been much faster than that of civilian employment;

TABLE III

Changes in Distribution of the Employed Work
Force by Sector, 1975 to 1981
(in millions)

	North America	OECD Europe
Agriculture	0.0	−2.3
Industry	4.8	−3.0
Services	10.5	6.1

Source: Employment Outlook, OECD, September 1983.

TABLE IV

Trends in Civilian and Government Employment
(average annual percentage rates of change)

	United States		European Economic Community	
	Civilian employment	Government employment	Civilian employment	Government employment
1968-1973	3.0	0.7	0.5	2.3
1973-1981	2.1	1.3	0.1	1.7

Source: Historical Statistics, OECD, 1983.

on the other hand, in the United States civilian employment growth has been systematically more rapid than that in the government sector. Thus it was the rapid rate of growth of employment in the public sector that permitted the EEC countries to avoid a serious worsening in the job market. One may nevertheless ask whether this development will not constitute an additional handicap for them in the future: public sector employment represents an overhead cost, the financing of which is a burden on the economy, particularly the private sector.

It is often stated, at least in Europe, that the development of *part-time jobs* can contribute to an increase in employment and to the reduction of unemployment. Table V offers some useful data on this question.

TABLE V

Part-Time Employment

	Part-time work as a percentage of total employment		Respective contributions of part-time and full-time work to employment changes, 1973 to 1981 (thousands)	
	1973	1981	Full-time	Part-time
United States	13.9	14.4	10,274	2,158
West Germany	7.7	10.2	−270	685
Great Britain	15.3	15.4	−626	−86
France	5.1	7.4	493	540

Source: Employment Outlook, OECD, September 1983.

The table shows a new and important difference between the United States and European countries. In the United States, from 1973 to 1981, new jobs have essentially been full-time jobs. In Europe nearly one new job out of every two was a part-time job and in West Germany, the significant growth in this type of employment compensated for a net decrease in full-time jobs.

The contribution of part-time work to the reduction of unemployment appears therefore to be dubious. In the United States, where part-time work contributed the least, total employment grew the most. In West Germany part-time employment was significant, yet the unemployment rate climbed no less than it did in France, where part-time jobs were less important. In Great Britain recourse to part-time employment is most widespread, yet the unemployment rate there is the highest.

In light of these data, it does not seem that part-time work has played a determining role in the creation of jobs or in the growth of unemployment. The reason seems to be that part-time work is not deliberately desired by workers. According to a number of European studies, the proportion of involuntary part-time work has increased during the last ten years.

Nonetheless, part-time work ought to be facilitated and encouraged since it helps to increase the flexibility of the labor market and to diversify the jobs made available to the work force. This is what the U.S. experience suggests. But the situation in Great Britain clearly shows that, even when it is widespread, part-time work does not suffice by itself to assure a satisfactory functioning of the labor market.

The length of the workweek has been diminishing in Europe, as in the United States, for many years. But recently the rates of decline have been different. Between 1976 and 1981, the length of the workweek diminished by 1.8 percent in the United States as compared to 8.2 percent in Great Britain, 5.9 percent in the Federal Republic of Germany and 2.8 percent in France. In the latter country a one-hour reduction in the workweek was imposed by law in January 1982.

It is interesting to note that there is no correlation between the length of the workweek and the number of jobs created, as is sometimes claimed. Indeed, it is in the United States, where the reduction in the length of the workweek is the smallest, that employment has increased the most rapidly. This is confirmed by the

Japanese experience since 1977, where the hours worked have increased while employment has grown (at a slower rate, to be sure, than in North America, but faster than in Europe). We might also cite the case of Belgium: among European nations, it is the one where the duration of the workweek has decreased the most during recent years and which has currently the shortest workweek. Yet it is experiencing the most serious employment problems.

Some Characteristics of *Unemployment* in the United States and Europe

If unemployment rates in Europe and the United States are comparable, the characteristics of joblessness differ considerably between the two regions with respect to two fundamental points: (1) unemployment among youth; and (2) the length of unemployment.

Unemployment among youth is a phenomenon common to both the United States and Europe. But, while in the United States the ratio between the unemployment rates of youth and adults declined between 1973 and 1982 (from 3.2 to 2.3 percent), it increased noticeably in the European countries (from 2.3 to 3.7 percent in France; from 1.3 to 1.8 percent in West Germany; and from 1.4 to 2.4 percent in Great Britain). Doubtless, this divergent evolution has multiple causes, but one in particular deserves mention: when the labor market declines significantly, unemployment increases more rapidly for adults as a whole than for women and youth; when the labor market improves, the opposite phenomenon occurs. In the light of the data presented above, we can say that between 1973 and 1982 the job situation in the United States should have deteriorated more than it did or, more precisely, that unemployment struck proportionately harder at skilled and experienced labor. An examination of the length of unemployment would provide still another corroborating index.

Among the possible causes of these phenomena are the rigidity of legal enactments guaranteeing employment security and minimum wage levels that are higher in Europe than in the United States, the impact of which is to hamper the employment of youth.

The length of unemployment is what differentiates the situation in European countries from that of the United States. Because of the lack of data directly comparing the length of unemployment between countries, we shall limit ourselves to a comparison of the number of long-term unemployed with the total number of unemployed.

It is apparent from Table VI that the increase in long-term unemployment is general. The phenomenon is particularly worrisome, not only because it profoundly affects the psychological condition and the material resources of those involved, but also because employers hesitate to hire jobless people who have been unemployed for a long time. The probability that a person will find a job diminishes as the length of his joblessness increases.

Long-term unemployment is more prevalent in European nations than in the United States. This is due to various factors in the United States: a more fluid labor market; more frequent labor-force dismissals to cope with temporary difficulties; more numerous employment opportunities; greater labor mobility, both professionally and geographically; and less comprehensive and less generous unemployment insurance.

But employment as a whole is less stable in the United States than in Europe, and the probability of being unemployed is markedly greater. On the other hand, the chances of finding a job or going back to work again are also higher.

Both in Europe and the United States an important and, without doubt, *a growing part of unemployment is structural*: the jobless cannot be absorbed into the labor market even in a period of high economic activity. According to the *Economic Report of the President* issued in February 1983, structural unemployment, defined as the

TABLE VI

Long-Term Unemployment (12 months or
more) as a Percentage of Overall
Unemployment

	1973	1982
United States	3.3	7.7
West Germany	8.5	21.2
Great Britain	26.9	33.3
France	21.6	39.8

Source: Employment Outlook, OECD, September 1983.

level of unemployment below which inflation tends to increase ("the inflation threshold unemployment rate"), is today around six to seven percent of the U.S. work force. We do not have comparable statistics for the countries of Europe; the rate of structural unemployment can be assumed to be similar.

The causes of structural unemployment are only partly common to the United States and Europe: lack of professional training of youth; the difficulty of retraining older workers; more generally, the failure of job seekers to qualify for jobs offered. In the United States, the rapid growth of the work force is a factor contributing to higher structural unemployment; in Europe, the lack of sufficient flexibility in the labor market is a determinant of structural unemployment.

In this connection, one should note the important effect of unemployment insurance on the duration and, in consequence, on the amount of structural unemployment in Europe. A similar observation may be made on the effect of the guaranteed minimum wage. These observations are not intended to criticize the principles of unemployment insurance or of minimum wages, which constitute irreversible social entitlements in Europe. Instead they are intended to point out that such measures of social progress can diminish the propensity of firms to hire labor, increase their propensity to fire, and lead to a growth in total measured unemployment. Thus, one cannot fail to connect the fact that before the reform of November 1982 France had the most generous system of unemployment insurance of the major developed nations with the fact that France was also the country with the highest proportion of long-term unemployed. In the United States, by contrast, the small proportion of long-term unemployed may in part be explained by the relative moderation of unemployment assistance.

II. Factors Determining Employment and Unemployment

The deterioration in the employment situation and the growth of joblessness is caused fundamentally, in Europe as in the United States, by the slowdown in economic expansion. But trends in wages and the profitability of invested capital aggravate employment problems in European countries. These countries must also deal with decay in some industries that have played an important economic and regional role in past decades.

The Slowdown in Expansion and Investment

Since 1975 the annual growth of the gross domestic product (GDP) has been on the average slower in Europe than in the United States: 2 percent as against 2.6 percent (Table VII).

Other things being equal, this fact alone is enough to explain why the growth of employment in Europe has been less rapid.

The different crises which have shaken the world economy since 1973—oil shocks, steep increases in the prices of other raw materials, a slowdown and then a contraction in world trade, international monetary disorders—have affected Europe more than the United States. Europe is poor in raw materials, depends more on foreign trade, and is more vulnerable to international competition. In addition, despite all the progress toward economic and monetary union, the EEC countries are not yet benefiting from all the advantages provided by the size of their domestic market, the availability of extensive financing resources, and a single, common currency. For these different reasons, America has weathered the effects of the world economic crisis better than Europe, and its prospects for growth and jobs are more favorable.

The slowdown in the growth of production has been accompanied by a more pronounced slowdown in investment. The share of investment in the GDP declined between 1974 and 1983 from 13.8 to 6.9 percent in France, from 10.4 to 7.3 percent in West

TABLE VII

Trend of the Gross Domestic Product
(average annual rate of increase in %)

	1960-1967	1967-1973	1973-1975	1975-1983
European Economic Community	4.4	5.0	0.2	2.0
United States	4.6	3.6	−0.8	2.6

Sources: Historical Statistics, OECD, 1983; *Economic Outlook,* OECD, December 1983.

Germany, from 9.5 to 4.3 percent in Great Britain, and on the average from 12.0 to 6.7 percent in the EEC. Compared to investment in the United States, the pattern in Europe has lasted longer, and the falloff in investment has been sharper. This situation has three serious effects upon employment: it keeps economic activity at its present weak level; it compromises future productive potential; and it affects adversely the international competitiveness of Community enterprises.

This latter point is particularly worrying. During the 1970s the competitiveness of European firms deteriorated. On the average, unit wage costs increased faster than among their competitors. In addition, the nominal average exchange rate for the EEC countries appreciated somewhat between 1973 and 1980. This conjunction of factors contributed to European employment difficulties and continued to be felt in 1982 and 1983.

Weakness in growth, accompanied by the relatively rapid increase in the work force, helps explain the softening in the labor market. The size of the labor force is increasing less rapidly in Europe than in the United States. Nonetheless, in a stagnating economic context, the growth of the work force in Europe is exceeding job availability.

Productivity and the Cost of Labor

Labor productivity has increased more rapidly in Europe than in the United States (averaging 2.1 percent since 1976 in Europe as against 0.5 percent in the United States). This is due to a number of factors. American industry, on the whole, has suffered less than European firms from the world crisis and has not had to endure such tight constraints to assure its survival. European firms, if they want to avoid going under and to recover international competitiveness, have no other alternative than vigorously to seek to achieve productivity gains. A precise comparison of the productivity trends in the United States and Europe would be necessary to understand this problem fully. The central fact is that since 1975 a sustained advance in productivity in Europe has been accompanied by a less sustained rate of growth. This explains the weakness in job creation as compared to the situation in the United States.

Another negative factor is the trend in social overhead costs as reflected in wages. The upward trend in real wages relative to the growth of the real national product has been much more moderate in the United States than in the EEC. This may be explained in part by the regions' differing gains in productivity. One may advance the hypothesis that the rapid increase in wages in Europe accounts for the relatively rapid gains in apparent labor productivity. The rise in real wages tends to increase the relative cost of the labor factor and to accelerate the tendency to substitute capital for labor. If this hypothesis is valid, the weakness of productivity gains in the U.S. economy would represent less a loss of efficiency than a combining of the factors of production that favor employment.

The cost of labor has risen more rapidly in the EEC, a fact that constitutes, by comparison with the United States, an additional handicap to the creation of jobs. In turn, this handicap is aggravated by the evolution of public expenditures, which have increased more heavily in Europe than in the United States. The data in Table VIII do not reflect the distribution of expenditures between government and business, but there is good reason to think that American business has suffered less from this phenomenon than European business has.

Finally, the return on invested capital has declined in Europe, and this affects employment adversely. According to the Deutsches Institut für Wirtschaftsforschung, the rate of the net return on fixed capital in Europe declined on the average from 10.6 per-

TABLE VIII

Trends in Real Earnings and in Government Outlays

	United States		OECD Europe	
	1972	1981	1972	1981
Difference in trends in real hourly earnings in manufacturing and real GDP per person employed (100 in 1972)	100.0	93.0	100.0	107.4
Total government outlays as a % of GDP	32.0	35.4	39.9	50.0

Sources: *Economic Outlook*, OECD, December 1983; *Historical Statistics*, OECD, 1983.

TABLE IX

Net Operating Surplus as Percentage of Net
Value Added in Industry, Transport and
Communication (average)

	1968-1973	1974-1981
West Germany	27.2	22.2
France	26.6	21.5
United Kingdom	21.5	18.9
United States	20.5	21.9

Source: Historical Statistics, OECD, 1983.

cent between 1960 and 1973, to 5.9 percent between 1974 and
1980, and to 4 percent in 1981.[1] By contrast, the profitability of
U.S. firms did not suffer during the world economic crisis
(Table IX).

Declining Industries

Since the 1970s, industries that constituted the foundations of economic development in industrialized countries as far back as the
nineteenth century have decayed or regressed; among them are:
coal mining, steel, textiles, shipbuilding, and basic chemicals.

Irrespective of the general economic slowdown, technological
change and the emergence of dynamic competitors in newly industrialized countries have deeply weakened the firms operating
in those sectors of industrialized countries and imposed on them a
choice between painful adaptation or elimination. The level of
employment has been severely reduced in given regions.

The situation is more worrisome in the European countries than
in the United States because in Europe traditional industries carry
more weight in the economy. Their geographical concentration has
generated a social environment that is unfavorable to mobility.
Moreover, European countries have not benefited on the whole
from the discovery of new sources of primary products or energy.

---

[1] Commission des Communautés Européennes, Economie Européenne, No. 18, November 1983, p. 84.

Finally, maintenance of financial and social benefits to workers in European industries has pushed up production costs beyond market prices.

It is obvious that these traditional industries, even if they succeed in adapting to competition, will not in the future offer as many jobs as in the past, and that new jobs will be generated by the service sector and by high-tech industries.

In summary, the above analysis suggests that both the United States and Europe will have to face some lasting difficulties with respect to unemployment. In both cases, the sharp slowing down of growth that has taken place since the first oil shock produced deleterious effects on the labor market. However, it seems that the disequilibrium in the U.S. labor market is essentially due to the rapid growth of the work force and to the instability of employment, while in Europe it is due to the weakness in the capacity to create jobs and in the excessive rigidity of adjustment mechanisms in the labor market.

In the United States economic growth occurred with a weak increase in per capita real income and in labor productivity and with vigorous growth in the number of persons employed. In Europe, on the contrary, it occurred with a rapid increase in productivity and per capita real income and with a relatively slower growth in employment. One may offer two reasons for this phenomenon. On the one hand, at the end of World War II, Europe had to make up for its technological lag. It did so, profiting at the same time from the need to rebuild its production system and install the most up-to-date equipment. On the other hand, until the mid-1970s Europe suffered from serious labor shortages—a fact that explains its reliance on immigrants and the choice of a development policy based on the intensive substitution of capital for labor. Nonetheless, a condition of chronic overemployment persisted until the beginning of the decade of the 1970s; this provoked lasting tensions among wage earners. The postwar quarter of a century profoundly marked the behavior and the mentalities of business managers and workers.

Today Europe has to deal with a relative abundance of manpower. If it does not modify the way it combines the factors of production so as to encourage employment, it will face grave difficulties. Such adaptation presupposes strong incentives for the creation of small and medium-sized firms, a modification of hiring procedures by employers, changes in labor's strategy in wage negotiations and in worker attitudes toward geographical and professional mobility.

III. Problems of National Economic Policy and International Economic Cooperation

Growth Policies

Nobody questions that the reduction of unemployment in Europe and in the United States depends principally on economic recovery and the renewal of economic growth.

The increase in unemployment in recent years explains why an economic policy tending to stimulate economic activity along post-Keynesian lines has been advocated in some European circles.

The French Socialist government adopted such a policy in June 1981. It increased the deficit of the French budget massively, from 1.2 percent to 3 percent of the GDP. It stimulated consumption by raising minimum wages, family allowances, and transfer payments (e.g., welfare), while it introduced very tight exchange-control regulations in order to limit the flight of capital and safeguard the value of the currency. The government decided to hire 200,000 additional civil servants, to reduce by one hour the duration of the workweek, to grant to all workers a fifth holiday week, and to encourage early retirement. The Socialists called these measures the "social treatment of unemployment."

This policy failed very quickly: in June 1982 the devaluation of the French franc, provoked by strong inflationary pressures and by a very sharp deterioration of the balance of payments, led the government to introduce price and wage controls and to slow the rise in public expenditures. A more rigorous austerity policy was introduced in April 1983 after the third devaluation of the French franc in less than two years; it resulted in a stagnation of economic activity and an increase in unemployment. The failure of the French Socialist policy has been partly attributed to the fact that no country can carry out a growth policy alone in an international environment characterized by stagnation or recession because it will inevitably incur a large external deficit that cannot be indefinitely financed by borrowing abroad and that sooner or later gives way to a policy of restricting demand.

Is it possible to avoid these consequences by obtaining the implementation of a coordinated growth policy from a group of countries? Is it possible to develop such a policy within the EEC or among the industrialized OECD countries?

Theoretically, all of this is possible; in practice things are not so easy. The main reason many European countries, first and foremost the Federal Republic of Germany, refused to participate in a coordinated growth policy was that they had to contend with serious imbalances and they wanted to achieve greater stability in order to build further growth on a sound basis. The "locomotive theory" advanced by the OECD in 1978 and accepted by the West German government did not bring convincing results and worsened the Federal Republic's budgetary problems. In 1979 the economic situation changed drastically. The Federal Reserve Board adopted a vigorous monetary policy and maintained it—rightly in my opinion—in order to break the back of inflation in the United States. After the second oil shock, all industrialized countries implemented adjustment policies that were more rigorous than those put in place after the first oil shock. They understood that it was no longer possible to defer adjustment and that if an increase in unemployment was the price to be paid for restoring stability, stability would pave the way to growth and a more satisfactory level of employment.

The current situation of the European countries clearly shows what are the main obstacles to a "growth policy."

The most important—domestically—is the budget deficit. It is very high in every EEC country because of a steady increase in government spending (from 49 percent of GDP in 1981 to 51 percent in 1983) and a decrease in revenues due to the recession. The increasing weight of interest on the public debt (0.8 percent of the GDP from 1981 to 1983 for the whole of the EEC; more than double this amount for Belgium, Denmark, Ireland and Italy) has compelled all the governments, anxious to stabilize their deficits, to increase taxes and to cut back on other government expenses. As a result, the nations with a low inflation rate are unable to exploit this advantage. Governments cannot reduce taxes or increase public expenditures to stimulate economic activity. Their priority is to stabilize, then to reduce the budget deficit, in order to reduce the borrowing needs of the public sector and limit the pressure of taxes on businesses and households.

The public finance strategy engaged in by most of the European governments is designed to reduce the weight of the public sector on the economy and to permit the private sector to benefit from a larger proportion of economic resources. A reduction of the budget deficit permits an easing of fiscal pressure and offers greater opportunities for private investment. A stricter control of public finances allows central banks to pursue a more flexible monetary policy. In the Federal Republic of Germany, the authorities have embarked on a vigorous effort to limit the growth in government spending to 2 percent and to reduce the net financing needs of all the public administrations from 3.1 percent of GDP in 1983 to 2.2 percent in 1984. The results of this policy appeared very encouraging at the beginning of 1984.

Difficulties also result from international constraints, i.e., the consequences of U.S. economic policy relating to interest rates and exchange rates.

Increases in interest rates—or keeping them at high levels—have been forced upon European economies by high rates in the United States and by the rapid rise in the value of the dollar, which is in part the result of those high rates. European monetary authorities have had to prevent too great a depreciation of their currencies as well as an outflow of capital to the United States.

The rise in the cost of borrowing money has weakened investment prospects. It is, moreover, reflected in the sharp increase in the real average interest rate paid on the public debt. If nominal interest rates have declined in a number of EEC countries (14.3 percent to 10.5 percent from January 1982 to September 1983 for short-term rates; a decline of 2.5 points on the average for long-term rates within the EEC), real interest rates, on the other hand, remain high (the yield on government bonds in West Germany is 5 percent and in the United Kingdom, 6.5 percent).

One must also take into account the indirect effects of the increase in U.S. interest rates on the EEC countries through the decline in the imports of developing countries. The less-developed countries must engage in restrictive import policies because of their debt problem. It is currently recognized that if there is a two point decline in demand on world markets, the GDP of the Community falls 0.5 percent in the following year; the contraction approaches 1 percent, if the decline is maintained.

Finally, if the rise in the value of the dollar is advantageous to EEC exports, it also has negative effects on European economies—on the one hand, increased prices of imports and, consequently increased costs of production, and on the other hand, an outflow of capital into dollar investment, which diminishes the financial resources available for European economies.

American-European relations are affected by the feeling, widely shared in Europe, that the United States has not properly assumed its responsibilities as the most powerful economy in the world. Even if many Europeans objectively recognize that the U.S. budget deficit is not the single cause of Europe's difficulties, they cannot help thinking that a better policy mix in the United States might lead to a fall in interest rates and reduce the overvaluation of the dollar. These developments would be beneficial to other advanced and developing countries. Electoral wait-and-see policy, which is attributed sometimes to the president and sometimes to Congress, cannot be regarded as a justification.

Since I am personally convinced that a lower rate of inflation, expansion of the U.S. economy, and a strong dollar are the major contributions the United States can make to a satisfactory working of the international economy, I deeply regret that the U.S. budgetary policy remains in such bad shape, with probable negative consequences in the medium term both for the United States and for the rest of the world.

A closer convergence in the economic policies of the industrialized countries is a condition for a long-lasting expansion in world economic activity. This depends above all upon the implementation in every industrialized country, and first of all in the United States, of coherent monetary, budgetary and exchange-rate policies aimed at balanced growth. It depends upon regional efforts to create areas of economic and monetary stability. It depends upon the attention all countries pay to their exchange rates in order to edge toward slightly greater monetary stability in the world. Intervention by central banks remains a useful policy instrument to offer the lead when markets have become disorderly or when movements differ greatly from those warranted by fundamental factors. As one central banker said, "Benign neglect does not have benign results, but rather may result in disorder." The progress in the coordination of economic policies among EEC countries and the strengthening of the European Monetary System, are very useful contributions to greater stability in the world.

International institutions can play an important role in the process of convergence and coordination of economic policies. They can offer objective explanations to national public opinion. They can give useful warning and assistance to governments that are not sufficiently aware of some dangerous trends or that do not face domestic difficulties in implementing appropriate policies; they can reduce conflicts of interest between their members and help make satisfactory solutions prevail. But it would be, in my opinion, rather illusory to attribute to them a greater influence than they actually have. International institutions remain, in the end, severely limited by national sovereignty.

The Temptation of Protectionism

If macroeconomics has its limits, would protectionism reduce the pressure of heavy unemployment? Until now there has been no serious movement in Europe either from political or trade-union circles in favor of jettisoning the relatively open trading system. Every government of an industrialized nation is aware of the grave risks that would come in the wake of a rejection of free trade. But the temptation is great for some, both in Europe and in the United States, to resort to specific measures or policies which, although ostensibly designed to facilitate a transition and to avoid serious social difficulties, would interfere with free trade.

If direct interference is rare, many measures supposedly designed to achieve other objectives do, in effect, constitute a disguised but not negligible form of protectionism.

Up to now, restrictions on imports and, in particular, the recourse to voluntary restrictions have been limited to those products or to those difficult situations in which the disorganization of the market risks the disruption of an activity on a big scale. Thus far, the few voluntary restrictive accords have not resulted in a significant contraction of world trade as a whole. But among certain governments, the temptation is present, given the difficulties encountered by certain enterprises or certain sectors of the economy, to maintain and increase protectionist devices in order to escape or postpone the real problems of structural adaptation.

More disturbing are current practices, such as subsidies or aid ostensibly given to further objectives of industrial development policy or to promote exports, that may end up either sustaining unproductive employment in traditional industries or in creating noncompetitive jobs in new industries under the cover of promoting up-to-date industrial policies.

If it is legitimate for every government to promote the harmonious development of all its nation's economic interests, this effort should not cause it to reject international competition. For such a rejection leads, after a brief decline in unemployment, to a falloff in economic growth and consequently in employment, with a waste of financial, material and human resources.

In some cases structural adaptation can require, for social and regional reasons, some protectionist measures or some specific financial assistance to firms: such measures can be useful only if they are transitory, degressive over a specified period of time, and closely linked to a restructuring program leading to international competitiveness. Such measures have to be discussed among international partners in order to be mutually acceptable and avoid retaliation.

Finally, policies designed to control exchange markets and the measures to carry them out provide governments with a weapon that is all the more effective because it is discreet and little subject to international challenge. Such policies permit the practice of a de facto protectionism that enables a country to escape the effects of international competition. International monetary cooperation, on a regional or international basis, should aim to prevent competitive devaluations and beggar-thy-neighbor policies.

The threat of protectionism has until now been averted thanks to the resistance of Western governments and the vigilant action of GATT (General Agreement on Tariffs and Trade). The U.S. attitude will be determining in this respect. If, under the influence of the various pressures making themselves felt in the United States, the American government were to adopt protectionist measures for important sectors of the U.S. economy, it would touch off vigorous reactions in Europe and oblige European governments to take retaliatory measures. It would be impossible for the Europeans to withstand the demands for protection from every quarter.

The heavy U.S. trade deficit can be considered a contribution to world recovery only if it does not lead to protectionist demands in the country. Such an outcome can also result from the overvaluation of the dollar. Thus a better policy mix in the United States appears to be a decisive factor in bringing about a sustained worldwide expansion.

The Mirage of an "Industrial Policy"

In some European countries as in the United States, a new instrument is being proposed to stimulate growth and create jobs: industrial policy. Such a policy would consist of two types of action by a government:

—nationalizing certain industries that are key to the development of the economy, especially high technology industries, in order to give them the financial resources necessary for research and investment;

—elaborating a strategy to guide the direction in which industrial structures ought to evolve, organizing the patterns of investment linked to this strategy, and taking appropriate measures to channel the flow of financial resources toward specific industries or firms.

Additional measures would, on the one hand, provide investment subsidies, research support, and trade protection to existing firms or to those just entering industries with high growth potential; and on the other, rehabilitate declining industries by creating barriers against imports and by providing special taxation and financial assistance.

The adoption of industrial policies could be a mistake. European experience in various countries shows very clearly that nationalized firms lose money, that their efficiency is lower than that of private firms, that the politicization of management and industrial relations is detrimental to their success. The basic reason for their lower efficiency is the absence of financial constraints, since the management of the firm is sure it can count on state subsidies or special financial assistance for its investment projects. In spite of that, nationalized firms cannot maintain a guarantee of employment to their workers indefinitely.

Nor is it easy to identify "strategic industries" or "winners" because it is so difficult to find objective criteria. Charles Schultze has rightly stated that "The competence, knowledge, and specific attributes that go with successful entrepreneurship and export capability are so narrowly defined and so fine-grained that they cannot be assigned to any particular nation."[2]

As for declining industries, it is better to reduce the transitional costs of adaptation than to try to slow the dynamic process of change and the growth of the economy.

Industrial policy runs the risk of being too costly and disappointing. On the other hand, dynamic economies need an overall policy for corporations that creates an environment favorable both to the development of new and rapidly expanding lines of activity and to the adaptability of firms to changing forms of competition. This is a rewarding contribution to high employment.

Promoting Employment

Macroeconomic policy in EEC countries is generally supplemented by an active employment policy designed to correct the structural causes of unemployment.

A notable effort has been undertaken in several countries to moderate the growth of wage costs so as to restore the international competiveness of firms and to increase their financial resources. This includes: reconsideration of wage indexation (Italy, Belgium and Holland); salary cuts or freezes for government employees (West Germany, Holland and Great Britain); and adoption of an incomes policy (France).

By these various methods, European governments are trying to impose a much stricter discipline with respect to real and nominal wage costs. From the high rate of an 11.5 percent salary increase in 1981, the average wage cost fell, according to estimates, to 7.2 percent in 1983.

---

[2] "Industrial Policy: A Dissent," *The Brookings Review*, Fall 1983, p. 8.

Incomes policy is effective when it is not a substitute for restrictive monetary and budgetary policies; it needs trade union support, but sooner or later can be undermined by new wage claims that can provoke a dangerous distortion of the economy. It does not work as a long-term policy device, except perhaps as a set of general guidelines.

Because of the difficulties encountered in retraining long-term unemployed older than 54, early retirement and pre-retirement systems have been created. They make it possible to avoid firing older workers who find it difficult to secure new employment, and they free jobs for younger workers. These systems are costly and impose an increasing burden on the social budget of the nation: their limits are rather quickly reached. They also have the serious drawback of increasing the ratio of retirees in the work force population of European countries, particularly from 1986 on. From that year the work force population (aged from 15 to 64) will stop growing; by contrast, the number of aged will increase rapidly.

A strong movement is developing among trade unions, as well as in certain political circles in the EEC, to alleviate the burden of unemployment by reorganizing and reducing the length of the workweek. It is certain that greater use of part-time work would increase the supply of labor and would specifically suit female job seekers. But it is not clear what the net impact on job creation would be.

But the demand most often heard is that of "work sharing." For example, in the Netherlands and Belgium, agreements between firms and trade unions have reduced the workweek from 40 to 38 or 36 hours. In France, it has been reduced by law to 39 hours. The West German trade unions have just demanded a 35 hour workweek.

Measures of this type will not lead to an increase in employment if they result in increased business costs. They should therefore meet a number of conditions:

—They should not be employed uniformly in all enterprises but should be the subject of negotiations which take account of the differences in given situations. Work sharing must accompany, and to a degree be determined by, "income sharing."

—The reduction in the hours of labor should be supplemented by measures permitting a better utilization of productive equipment.

—The reduction in work time must take account of the flexibility required by certain industries.

Reduction in the hours of labor must be practiced with care insofar as it might weaken the competitiveness of European industry vis-à-vis U.S. and Japanese industry.

To reduce the structural component of unemployment, government policies should try to increase the mobility of labor and eliminate the rigidities and constraints which make enterprises hesitate to hire workers.

In many European countries, small business has a considerable potential for hiring labor. Consequently, programs helping create small businesses or create additional jobs in small businesses or artisanal enterprises are particularly opportune. Programs of this kind not only provide financing but also ease the fiscal and administrative constraints affecting these enterprises. Thus it is possible at one and the same time to develop employment and hinder the growth of a black market economy.

IV. Conclusion

In European countries, the unemployment problem is linked to two ongoing processes: one of cyclical adjustment and one of structural adaptation. They both take time. Public opinion—allowed for too long to expect a rapid end to the crisis—has begun to realize, and to accept, the necessary sacrifices. As a result, the political tensions stemming from the rapid growth of unemployment are more moderate than expected. If unemployment stirs great anxiety among peoples long used to full employment, it no longer ought to cause deep social and political disturbances, even if a climate of uncertainty and worry is widespread.

In this connection, the French Socialist experience has served to create awareness of the restrictions that need to be accepted and of the errors to be avoided. The failure of the Socialist policy of economic stimulation and the drastic changes in the goverment's strategy have educated public opinion, not only in France, but also in a number of other European countries where socialists have come to power (Spain and Italy, in particular). In other countries, such as Great Britain and the Federal Republic of Germany, election victories by conservative and liberal parties demonstrate clearly that public opinion no longer believes in the "magical recipes" that had been recommended to reduce unemployment.

In the future, even if Europe again finds the way to growth and prosperity, it will have to live with higher unemployment rates than those it has known for the last 20 years. The amount of joblessness that will prevail will depend, first, on the adaptability of production structures to the new conditions of international competition; second, on the growth in the flexibility of the labor market; and above all, on an intense individual and collective effort to increase the productivity and competitiveness of the European economies.

In the years ahead European governments will have to manage their economies with great care. They cannot finance unlimited budget and balance-of-payments deficits, principally because they do not have the power to create an internationally accepted currency. Hence they have to maintain a medium-term financial strategy that permits a reduction in the public-sector burden and limits national borrowing needs. They also have to avoid at any price protectionist policies that diminish productivity, weaken the competitiveness of their firms in foreign markets, and slow down their economies.

Cooperation among all industrialized countries would be helpful; this requires international management. But the fundamental necessity is the national will in every country to maintain conditions required for balanced growth and international competitiveness.

James Tobin

Unemployment in the 1980s: Macroeconomic Diagnosis and Prescription

I. Unemployment and Aggregate Demand

Unemployment in the 24 nations of the Organization for Economic Cooperation and Development (OECD) rose from 5.5 percent of the labor force in 1979 to 10 percent in 1983. The number of unemployed persons rose from 18 million to 32 million. This development was the second upward ratchet in unemployment in the decade following the first oil shock. (Table I summarizes the recent history of unemployment in the advanced economies of the noncommunist world.)

The prospects of reducing unemployment to 1979 rates, let alone 1973 rates, are dismal for the remainder of the 1980s. For the governments of the major locomotives of the world economy—the seven countries of the annual economic summit conferences (Canada, France, West Germany, Italy, Japan, the United Kingdom, and the United States)—significant reduction of unemployment is not a high joint or individual priority. Nor is it apparently a big concern of the electorates of these democracies. The prevailing attitudes, among both governors and governed, are fatalism and complacency; not much can be done, not much needs to be done, about unemployment. The fiscal and financial plans of most governments contemplate adjustment to permanently higher unemployment rates.

Europeans seem more resigned to the intractability of unemployment than North Americans. In the United States, return to unemployment rates less than a point above those of 1978 and 1979 is considered possible and desirable. The strong economic recovery which began in mid-1982 buoyed optimism on this side of the Atlantic; unemployment has subsided from a cyclical peak of 10.7 percent in December 1982 to 7.8 percent in February 1984.

79

TABLE I Selected Macroeconomic Data for OECD Economies

	(a) Unemployment Rates (%) (average for year)			(b) Capacity Utilization Indexes		
	1973	1979	1983	1973	1979	1983
United States	4.8	5.8	9.5	88	86	75
Japan	1.3	2.1	2.7	100	90	83
West Germany	0.8	3.2	8.5	87	84	78
France	2.6	5.9	8.3	85	82	77
United Kingdom	3.3	5.6	11.5	43	42	32
Seven summit countries	3.4	5.0	8.3			
Fifteen OECD countries	3.3	5.1	9.0			

	(c) Real Growth (% per yr.) GNP or GDP			(d) Output Gap: % Shortfall of 1983 GNP/GDP below 1979, projected to 1983 by	
	1965-73	1973-79	1979-83	1973-79 trend	mean of 1973-79 and 1965-73 trends
United States	3.8	2.8	0.9	7.1	8.9
Japan	9.8	3.7	3.6	0	11.2
West Germany	4.1	2.4	0.5	7.5	10.4
France	5.2	3.1	1.1	7.7	11.3
United Kingdom	3.8	1.4	0	5.3	9.8
Seven summit countries					
Fifteen OECD countries					

	(e) Money Wage Inflation (%)			(f) Unit Labor Costs (% Increase over prev. yr.)		
	1973	1979	1983	1973	1979	1983
United States	7.1	8.4	4.6	3.4	6.9	3.7
Japan	23.4	7.4	4.5	2.3	−2.5	1.2
West Germany	10.7	5.5	2.7	5.4	2.0	−1.2
France	14.6	13.0	11.0	7.2	6.1	8.0
United Kingdom	12.7	15.5	8.0	5.4	12.8	1.2
Total OECD	13.0	9.6	6.0			
Seven summit countries				4.6	5.3	3.5

	(g) Price Inflation, GNP/GDP deflator (% rise over prev. yr.)		
	1973	1979	1983
United States	5.8	8.6	4.2
Japan	11.9	2.6	1.0
West Germany	6.5	4.1	3.0
France	7.1	10.4	9.0
United Kingdom	7.1	15.1	5.2
Total OECD		8.4	4.7
Seven summit countries		7.9	5.2

Recovery in Europe has been later and weaker; unemployment is still rising, and common projections envisage a "recovery" which leaves joblessness on a new higher plateau. Japan is a special case. Overt unemployment is always low, but the measured increases since 1973 and 1979 nonetheless are symptoms of large and growing margins of economic slack. Recent improvements in Europe and Japan reflect mainly export demands due directly or indirectly to the American recovery.

Half a century ago, four years of precipitous decline in world economic activity generated mass unemployment. Most of this persisted through the six years of recovery prior to the Second World War, which brought with it shortages of labor and everything else. The depression of 1979-83 was much less severe, and now society treats the jobless more generously than in the 1930s. Yet there are disturbing parallels. Then as now, governments and central banks eschewed active measures to create jobs in favor of austere fiscal and financial policies designed to win the confidence of international bankers and bond-holders. Their efforts, individually and collectively, made depression and unemployment worse; and in the end they failed to balance budgets, protect currency parities, or prevent exposed banks from falling like dominoes.[1] Chancellor Heinrich Bruning adhered religiously to the canons of

---

[1] For the tale well-told see Charles P. Kindleberger, *The World in Depression,* Berkeley: University of California Press, 1973, especially chapters 6 through 8 and 11. It should be required reading for the economic statespersons of the 1980s.

Notes: Except for the United States, figures for 1983 are OECD estimates from incomplete information. The seven summit countries include Italy and Canada. The fifteen OECD economies are the advanced countries, for which employment data are meaningful.

(a) Unemployment rates are standardized by OECD to United States definition.

(b) Estimates of utilization of manufacturing capacity. For Japan, the Ministry of International Trade and Industry index is normalized to 1973. For the United Kingdom, figures are percentages of firms reporting full utilization.

(e) Hourly earnings in manufacturing for the United States and West Germany. Monthly earnings for Japan. Weekly earnings for the United Kingdom. Hourly wage rates for France.

(f) Labor costs per unit of manufacturing output. For Germany, includes mining.

Sources: Economic Outlook, OECD, No. 27, July 1980 and No. 34, December 1983; *Main Economic Indicators,* OECD; *International Financial Statistics,* International Monetary Fund; and *Economic Report of the President,* 1984, U.S. Government Printing Office.

sound finance, and within a year after he left office, the Weimar Republic fell to Hitler. France, the leader of the gold bloc, eventually succumbed to the disasters it helped to inflict on its neighbors. Weakened by economic strife, political chaos, and class warfare throughout the 1930s, France was no match for Nazi Germany. Capitalism, democracy and Western civilization barely survived.

Such momentous dangers seem remote today. But passive acceptance of prolonged high unemployment cannot be taken for granted either. Another decade of poor economic performance can undermine allegiance to the institutions of democratic capitalism, especially among successive cohorts of youth who fail to find jobs. Macroeconomic disappointments can also erode support for the international economic and political order on which the security and prosperity of the free world have been based since 1945. They have already triggered autarkic measures and proposals in nearly every nation, *sauve qui peut* expedients that protect some jobs and businesses at the expense of others and sacrifice the gains from efficient trade in the process. Stagnation in the developed "North" is devastating to the less developed and debt-burdened "South." The austere prescriptions of the International Monetary Fund are politically risky in many countries friendly to the West. They may be inevitable when sick economies are treated one by one. But in aggregate the medicines, like the belt-tightening national policies of the Great Depression, make the world situation worse.[2] Moreover, neither the examples nor the effects of current performance and policies in the advanced countries are likely to win the contest for the hearts and minds of the Third World.

The Great Depression taught the world that mass unemployment in advanced capitalist economies was a *macroeconomic* problem. That revelation means several things: first, when millions of people become unemployed, it is not because of their individual characteristics. They have not suddenly become lazy or unruly or

---

[2] For analysis and projection of Third World debt problems, see William R. Cline, *International Debt and the Stability of the World Economy*, Washington, D.C.: Institute for International Economics, 1983. Cline shows how solvency depends on export volume and terms of trade highly sensitive to OECD economies' real growth, and on restoring a positive margin between debtor countries' export growth rates and the interest rates at which they borrow.

unproductive or untrainable. The jobs are just not there. When jobs reappeared in the late 1930s and the 1940s, as in all subsequent cyclical recoveries, the unemployed were willing and able to fill them.

Second, mass unemployment is not due to shortages of capital equipment, land or other productive resources complementary to human labor. Indeed, industrial capacity is underutilized too. Table I shows for the most recent decade how measures of capacity utilization have fallen while unemployment has risen.

Third, unemployment and underutilization of capacity both vary inversely with aggregate production and real income. This relation also is illustrated in Table I, where shortfalls of gross domestic product (GDP) from trend have risen parallel to unemployment.

Fourth, short-run fluctuations in production, employment and capacity utilization are principally fluctuations in aggregate demand for goods and services. Potential aggregate supply, the productive capacity of a national economy or group of national economies, varies little from year to year. Of course, supply is the determinative constraint over horizons longer than business cycles. Growth of productive capacity is the source of secular progress in standards of living.

Fifth, mass unemployment is not technological in origin. New technologies do, of course, displace particular workers and work hardships upon them, and upon whole industries and regions. But human labor in general has never yet become obsolete. Despite the dire science fiction prophecies that accompany every period of high unemployment, revival of aggregate demand has always created jobs in numbers vastly beyond the imaginations of the pessimists—or to put the point the other way round, productivity has not spurted to the heights imagined by the optimists. Given a buoyant macroeconomic climate, market capitalism has repeatedly demonstrated its capacity to adapt to new technologies, new patterns of demand, and new structures of comparative advantage in interregional and international trade.

Sixth, governments' monetary and fiscal policies are powerful influences on aggregate demand. They can be used to reduce unemployment due to deficiences of demand. After World War II, every economically advanced democracy resolved not to allow unemployment to become again the scourge it had been in the 1930s. The next quarter-century was an era of prosperity, growth and stability without parallel in economic history. Compared to prewar experience, even excluding the Great Depression of the 1930s, unemployment rates were low and fluctuated in a narrow band. The use of monetary and fiscal policies contributed to the favorable macroeconomic climate. The perverse policies so disastrous in the early 1930s were not repeated. But they are being repeated now.

Aside from its macroeconomic instruments, a modern democracy governing a decentralized economy has almost no tools to cope with unemployment. So-called structural, manpower or labor-market policies are by no means new. Almost every advanced country has pursued them for decades. They can, as their successful use in Sweden in particular suggests, smooth and speed movements of workers displaced by technological and industrial change to new jobs. They can, therefore, reduce the minimal frictional unemployment inevitable in a dynamic economy. But they cannot do so unless the jobs are there, and thus they are virtually helpless when the macroeconomic climate is inclement. They are a useful complement to, but no substitute for, macroeconomic policies that assure adequate effective demand.

To be sure, our governments have the responsibility to educate our youth, but one can scarcely argue that today's young people are more vulnerable to unemployment than their fathers and mothers were because they are less educated—the contrary is the truth. Government programs can train or retrain workers in skills relevant to contemporary technology and industrial practice. It is futile and even demoralizing if the graduates of those programs cannot be placed, or if they simply displace workers whom those programs passed by. In any case, evidence and common sense indicate that the best training is generally on-the-job experience itself. Governments can help to match job openings with available candidates by collecting and disseminating information on job specifications and workers' qualifications. But there is no reason to think that more than a tiny amount of unemployment is due to inefficiencies in these matchings at present. Nonetheless, there are vastly more unemployed than vacancies today. Governments can sharpen incentives for encouraging the unemployed to search for jobs and to accept less attractive offers by diminishing the compensation paid to them and by instituting other reforms. Several governments are currently doing just that. This may help, but the fact remains that low unemployment coexisted with generous unemployment compensation for a long time. Governments can spread more evenly the work opportunities available by encouraging or mandating shorter hours. This does not really reduce unemployment, except by the illusion of the statistical conventions that do not count persons involuntarily working short hours. A fairer distribution of the burdens may ease the pain to the affected workers, but it does not diminish the overall economic waste.

An all too common misconception about unemployment is that its social cost is negligible when the incomes of the unemployed themselves are substantially maintained by the welfare-state subventions to which they are entitled. For one thing, those payments are not compensation for the stigma and demoralization of enforced idleness in a society where achievement at work is a principal source of esteem and self-esteem. Economists are wrong to think that most people positively dislike work and engage in it only for the pay. In any case, the cost of unemployment and of excess capital capacity to the society is the shortfall of GDP. The lost output could have augmented private and public consumption or national wealth, either productive capital at home or net claims on the rest of the world. That loss is the burden; unemployment insurance and worksharing redistribute but do not eliminate it. The substantial size of the burden is shown in Table I, the percentage shortfalls of GDP from trend. Economists generally use the unemployment rate as a barometer of macroeconomic performance and of cyclical fluctuation. In this sense, reduction in unemployment is valued not just in itself but as the symptom of economy-wide gains of output and income.

Those who expect structural labor-market policies to make a significant dent in current unemployment are, I believe, whistling in the dark. Many who propose them are probably rationalizing conscious preferences for continued slack in labor markets. Macroeconomic stimulus is necessary to lower unemployment to rates comparable to those of the late 1970s. It is probably sufficient as well. Structural labor-market policies can make only marginal improvements.

A long-standing constraint in all advanced economies on the reduction of unemployment by expansion of aggregate demand for goods and services, whether from stimulative policies or from other internal or external sources, is the possible inflationary by-product of such expansion. The extents to which inflationary risks are, and can reasonably be, the basic reasons for the reluctance of major governments to employ their macroeconomic policy instruments to lower unemployment will be discussed below. Structural policies to diminish those risks and loosen the constraints they impose on macroeconomic policies will be discussed below as well. They are to be distinguished from direct labor-market policies.

II. Unemployment, the Permanent Cure for Inflation?

The principal intellectual obstacle to the use of policies of demand stimulus, monetary or fiscal, to reduce unemployment is fear of inflation. Demand management was discredited in the 1970s by the surges of inflation that terminated two cyclical recoveries in 1973-74 and 1979-80, recoveries driven or accommodated in degrees varying among countries by expansionary macroeconomic policies. The lesson learned by many policymakers, influential citizens, and economists is that unemployment cannot be cured in this way without unacceptable risk of inflation. This view is more solidly entrenched in Europe than in North America.

Reconciling high employment and price stability has been a chronic dilemma in advanced democratic economies for nearly four decades, most pronounced in the stagflationary decade of the 1970s. Economists generally recognize that the occurrence of price and wage acceleration at low rates of unemployment limits the possibility of reducing unemployment by management of aggregate demand. But to estimate where the limit is, to give a numerical value to the minimal inflation-safe unemployment rate for a specific economy at a specific time, is very difficult. The implicit consensus view of that threshold—often called the "natural rate" though there is not necessarily anything natural about it, some-

times called the "non-accelerating-inflation-rate-of-unemploy-
ment" or NAIRU—has appeared to rise secularly, for example, in
the United States from four percent in the 1960s to five percent in
the mid-1970s to six percent or higher now. (President Reagan's
Council of Economic Advisers pronounces it to be 6.5 percent for
the 1980s.) Governments and central banks who consider stability
of prices, or at least stability of low inflation rates, their paramount
goals, to which employment and production objectives are subordinate, are inclined to take no risk of crossing the threshold. In
this view they are supported by a new generation of anti-Keynes-
ian economists who believe essentially that labor markets are always in equilibrium, so that actual unemployment is always natural.

Over-learning the Lessons of the 1970s

The dismissal of expansionary macroeconomic policies is in my
opinion a misreading of, at least an overreaction to, the events of
the 1970s. The frightening inflations accompanied two external
price shocks without parallel in modern peacetime history. The
Yom Kippur War, the oil embargo, and the first Organization of
Petroleum Exporting Countries price hike (OPEC I) were not endogenous consequences of the 1971-73 recovery or of the major
policies that fostered it. The Ayatollah Khomeini, the Iran-Iraq
War, and OPEC II were not endogenous results of the recovery of
1975-79 or of the policies that supported it. Those two shocks
would have been seriously inflationary and stagflationary even if
demand policies had been more restrictive and unemployment
higher before, when and immediately after they occurred. This is
not to exonerate demand policies of all responsibility for the inflations of the 1970s. It is to say that those events tell us little about
the natural rate of unemployment and the safe limits of demand
expansion in the 1980s.

It is true that the growth of American oil demand after 1974,
due both to macroeconomic expansion and to continued controls
on domestic oil prices, helped to bring world oil demand into
collision with limits on OPEC's willing supply. It increased the
vulnerability of oil-importing economies to the political interrup-

tions of supply which occurred and to the hoarding of oil in anticipation of them. But if the inflation at the end of the 1970s tells us about any "natural" rate, it was not that of unemployment but of oil consumption at the time.

Today the oil and energy situation is much improved. Abundant new non-OPEC supplies are available. Oil producers both within and outside the cartel are pumping far below capacity and far below their desired rates of exploitation. Thanks to decontrol of prices by Presidents Carter and Reagan and to other incentives for conservation and substitution, Americans have, like consumers elsewhere, substantially reduced consumption of energy in general, and oil in particular. These improvements continue as producers and consumers put into use energy-efficient machinery, structure, and appliances. We have found less costly ways to economize petroleum than economy-wide, worldwide recession and stagnation. It is estimated that recovery will restore only one-quarter of Americans' reduction in oil consumption since 1979. A third oil shock cannot be ruled out, but we are much better prepared. It cannot make sense to run our economies at low speed permanently just because another oil shock would be somewhat less inflationary in those circumstances than if the world economy were prospering.

In other respects too the inflation outlook is pleasant. Table I includes figures showing the impressive progress in disinflation of prices and wages in the major economies. The hardships of the past four years did accomplish something. The considerable slack in all economies should continue to discipline wages and prices even while utilization rates improve. Growth of productivity is reviving and holding down unit labor costs.

The Classical Unemployment Diagnosis

In Europe the restrictive stance of macroeconomic policy in the face of the highest unemployment and deepest depression in half a century is rationalized by a pessimistic diagnosis of the maladies. They are not the type, it is argued, that management of demand can cure; hence expansionary fiscal and monetary stimuli will just be dissipated in inflation. In effect, the inflation threshold rate of unemployment is close to the current rate.

Specifically, the argument goes like this: in the jargon of economics, the unemployment is classical, not Keynesian, i.e., the culprit is not low demand but rigidly high real wages. Wage rates, relative to the prices employers receive for their products, are too high to make expansion of employment profitable. Trade union power, exercised on behalf of senior employees, defends uneconomically high real wages against the potential competition of the less privileged workers whom they render involuntarily unemployed. Raising markups and prices will not relieve the profit squeeze because money wage rates will promptly and fully follow prices up. The process may or may not be formalized by indexation; in either case, the convention that money wages should rise with the cost of living is strong. It is especially damaging to profit margins and employment when, as in the cases of oil price shocks or exchange depreciations, cost of living indexes are rising relative to the prices of local products. Unless the real wage impasse is broken, demand stimulus is impotent to raise employment and production. Misdiagnosing and treating unemployment as Keynesian will only release an inflationary wage-price spiral.

According to this theory, classical unemployment arose in Europe after the first oil shock.[3] Organized labor was accustomed to the pre-OPEC growth of real wages and resisted departure from the trend. But employers could no longer afford to pay those wages, and the "wage gap" grew as the growth of labor productivity slowed down. Countries like the United Kingdom, which nonetheless tried to restore high unemployment, suffered from inflation, while West Germany, the most important example, recognized the new situation and kept inflation under control. This scenario makes some sense through 1979 or even 1980 but strains credulity for the subsequent rise of unemployment. For the later

---

[3] Herbert Giersch, "Aspects of Growth, Structural Change, and Employment—A Schumpeterian Perspective," and Michael Bruno and Jeffrey Sachs, "Supply versus Demand Approaches to the Problem of Stagflation," in *Macroeconomic Policies for Growth and Stability: A European Perspective*, ed. Giersch, Symposium 1979, Tübingen: Mohr, for the Institut für Weltwirtschaft an der Universität Kiel, 1981.

period, structural disturbances due to new technology and foreign competition are said to have rendered much existing human and physical capital obsolete.

It is difficult to tell by inspection whether unemployment is Keynesian or classical, or in what proportions it is the one or the other. It is difficult to tell whether real wages are above those which would be consistent with a lower unemployment rate, and if they are, to say whether or not they would naturally fall during a demand-driven recovery. And even if all those doubts are resolved on the pessimistic, classical side, it is gratuitous to assume that governments can do nothing to modify the recalcitrant path of real wages.

Squeezed profit margins are characteristic of cyclical lows of business activity, and sometimes but not always reflect high real wages. Recoveries generally restore profit margins, and not necessarily by lowering real wages (relative to trend).

In retrospect no one doubts that mass unemployment in the 1930s was Keynesian. But an observer of the world scene in 1933 would have noted a severe profit squeeze. Real wages had risen in terms of labor's product from 1929 to 1932 in West Germany, Sweden and the United Kingdom; they had fallen in the United States. Labor's share of product had risen by 38 percent, 9 percent and 16 percent in the first three countries respectively, and also by 11 percent in the United States.[4] It would have been easy to call unemployment in the Great Depression classical. Indeed most economists rejected monetary and fiscal solutions at the time.

Keynes pointed out how real wages could be high and profits squeezed because of the same deficiency of aggregate demand that caused the unemployment.[5] In recession and depression businesses cut prices competitively but lay off workers and cut production until their (marginal) costs at existing wages are lowered as much as their prices. During reflations and recoveries they reverse

---

[4] Jeffrey D. Sachs, "Real Wages and Unemployment in the OECD Countries," *Brookings Papers on Economic Activity*, No.1, Washington, D.C.: Brookings Institution, 1983; Sheila Bonnell, "Real Wages and Employment in the Great Depression," *Economic Record*, September 1981, pp. 277-281.

[5] J. M. Keynes, *The General Theory of Employment, Interest, and Money*, New York: Harcourt, Brace & Co., 1936.

the process, enjoying higher profit margins as prices rise relative to wages, while increasing employment and production. Workers gladly accept additional employment even though their real wages may be falling. The Keynesian mechanism envisages cyclical price movements around relatively stable money wages. Keynesian adaptations of real wages occurred in the recoveries of the three European countries in the 1930s. In the United States real wages gained as production, employment and profits recovered.

Almost immediately after publication of the *General Theory*, empirical investigations challenged Keynes' unquestioning acceptance of the conventional view that real wages, because they must be equal to the marginal productivity of labor, will vary countercyclically.[6] Those and many subsequent studies concluded that both labor productivity and product-wages more usually rise than fall during cyclical upswings, as was true in the United States in the 1930s. The classical theory of marginal cost pricing is not a reliable guide to the cyclical behavior of prices and real wages. In an imperfectly competitive economy in disequilibrium, relief of profit squeeze is provided by higher volume, increasing returns to scale and efficient utilization of both overhead labor and redundant employees. As aggregate demand expansion shifts out firms' product demand curves, employers with constant or declining marginal costs will raise employment without any reduction of product wages.

For these reasons, observations of high real wages and squeezed profit margins do not per se show that unemployment is classical and not susceptible to Keynesian remedies. Rigidly high real wages may be the effective constraint on expansion of output and employment in particular economies in particular circumstances. Credible recent examples are the United Kingdom and Sweden in the 1970s, where export industries unprofitable at internationally competitive prices could not be made competitive by devaluation because of wage indexation. The immediate question is the applicability of the classical unemployment thesis to the "locomotive" economies today, discussed in the next section.

---

[6] J. T. Dunlop, "The Movement of Real and Money Wages," *Economic Journal*, No. 48, September 1938.

One other point of macroeconomic theory deserves emphasis. Even if real wage reduction is necessary for expansion of output and employment, it may not be sufficient. Suppose, for example, that workers economy-wide give up one annual cost-of-living increase of money wages to allow business profit margins to increase. The redistribution of purchasing power does not obviously increase aggregate demand, and may indeed diminish consumption. A positive outcome can come from net exports; this will benefit any one open economy at the expense of others, but it is not a solution for all countries together. In a closed economy, or in the world as a whole, the hope would center on business investment. Will it be encouraged enough by the improved outlook for profit margins to overcome the disincentives of current excess capacity and sales prospects? Maybe, if the profit improvement is expected to be permanent. Maybe not. The safest course would be to combine durable wage corrections with assurances of accommodative and, if necessary, stimulative demand policies.

Policies to Improve the Inflation-Unemployment Trade-off

By far the most formidable barrier to monetary and fiscal stimulus to recovery and jobs is the risk of reacceleration of wages and prices. The danger seems remote today, when OECD economies are performing so far below capacity. But any business cycle recovery raises some prices. The prices of raw materials and foodstuffs traded in world commodity markets, sensitive to demand and supply, fell precipitously in the recent depression. Flexible upwards too, they are bound to rise in recovery. Likewise, businesses will have to restore to normal profitable rates the mark-ups they shaved in hard times. These reversals are one-shot price increases, but they worsen month-to-month inflation statistics temporarily while they take place. Nervous policymakers cannot know for sure that they do not presage a more stubborn escalation of inflation.

Central banks and governments are so sensitized to inflationary dangers that they will resolve on the side of caution and restriction their uncertainties about the location of the minimal inflation-safe unemployment rate. They will buy insurance against a new spurt of inflation at the cost of extra points of unemployment. For their economies and the world, this insurance is very expensive. It may well be increasingly expensive, and ultimately self-defeating, in the long run. Experience suggests that prolonged high unemployment becomes "natural" and structural—a self-fulfilling prophecy. The mechanisms are obvious: unemployed workers lose, or never aquire, the skills and habits imbued by actual job experience. Businesses lack the profits and prospects that spur investments in new capacity and technology; the advance of productivity falters, and bottlenecks loom at ever higher unemployment rates.

The obvious desiderata are policies to diminish the inflation risks of demand expansion and to lower the inflation-safe unemployment rate. The candidates fall into two somewhat overlapping categories: *institutional reforms* and *incomes policies*. The prospects and the particulars differ widely from country to country. Here it is possible only to indicate general principles, with illustrative examples.

In most countries the institutions of wage- and price-setting are biased upwards. That is, wages and prices—other than those commodity prices set continuously by supply and demand in auction markets—rise more readily than they fall. Consider government-supported floors on farm prices, minimum wages, asymmetrical indexation. Consider the inexorable ascent of costs of health care, undisciplined by market forces when payments are by third-party insurers, governmental or private. Consider the limited sensitivity to excess capacity of "administered" industrial prices, and the stubbornness of negotiated wages in the face of unemployment. When government interventions are responsible for these biases, they are obvious, though politically elusive, targets of legislative reform. When governments grant private agents and groups—trade unions or trade associations—immunities from competition, the public has at the very least the right to insist that the privileges are not exercised in ways that inflict inflation or unemployment on the whole society. For example, if indexing is permitted at all, it should be symmetrical; and the price index used should exclude cost-of-living increases that are burdens to employers and to the whole society as well as to workers, like import price boosts and increased sales taxes.

In most countries, collective bargaining procedures are sanctioned, protected and regulated by legislation. A general problem is that no one represents workers laid off or never hired. All too often the wages of senior employed workers take precedence over the number of jobs. Remedies are hard to find. Perhaps official recognition as bargaining agents could be denied to unions that restrict membership and deny voice to the unemployed. Perhaps employers who raise wages while curtailing employment, or while qualified workers are in excess supply in their industry or region, should have to pay penalty surcharges into unemployment insurance funds. Perhaps legislation should provide incentive subsidies for employers and workers to agree on compensation systems which, like the Japanese model, condition some payments to workers on the profits or revenues or productivity gains of the firm.

Incomes policies are an alternative more readily available. In one form or another, they have on occasion been practiced by almost every country. They range from the full-blown detailed price and wage ceilings of wartime mobilization to advisory guideposts dependent on persuasive interventions by government leaders. In a sense, threats, promises and conditions respecting monetary and fiscal policies are also incomes policies. Their recent use in the United States and United Kingdom was not encouraging. They work better where wage bargains are synchronized in time, and in significant degree centralized; where government officials, union leaders and business representatives can annually discuss wage and price patterns in their macroeconomic contexts.

Explicit incomes policies have failed when they attempted to suppress inflation in overheated peacetime economies; when they were removed before inflation expectations were damped; when they lacked or lost the consensus of the parties; when they were overwhelmed by uncontrollable price shocks, as in the oil crises of the 1970s. Past failures have made incomes policies unfashionable, but *faute de mieux* they deserve to be reconsidered.

Today conditions are favorable in several major economies. There is plenty of economic slack; inflation and expectations of inflation have been receding; both workers and employers can see how much they have to gain from a sustained non-inflationary recovery. In similar circumstances from 1961 to 1965 the Kennedy-Johnson guideposts, though without the teeth of legal compulsion, helped to keep recovery free of inflation. Today they probably should be strengthened by incentives for compliance, either the stick of tax penalties or the carrot of tax rewards. Tax-based incomes policy (TIP) is designed for decentralized, unsynchronized institutions of wage- and price-setting, and designed to avoid the rigidities and inefficiencies of absolute controls. It may not be necessary in economies with institutions for economy-wide bargaining. Whatever the institutions and the policy, the indispensable ingredient is the leadership of presidents and prime ministers to develop and sustain the underlying consensus. Unfortunately, this leadership will never come from governments whose laissez-faire ideologies tell them that market economies will on their own achieve full employment without inflation—unless they define "full employment" tautologically as whatever unemployment occurs.

Ordinary citizens never believe economists and bankers who tell them unemployment is the only cure for inflation. They think there must be a better way, and they are right.

III. The Case for Demand Expansion in Europe and Japan

Among the seven summit countries, the United States, West Germany and Japan are the decisive actors in the macroeconomic drama. They have the opportunity and responsibility to restore prosperity and growth for the whole world. Canada must willy-nilly follow in the footsteps of its large neighbor to the south, amplifying its world impact. In Europe, West Germany is the key economy. Its macroeconomic performance and policy set the tone for the European Economic Community and for the whole area. Of the three other large economies of Western Europe, only the United Kingdom has much room for independent maneuver just now. France is still paying the penalties of deviating from the deflationist ranks of its trading partners in the first year of Mitterrand's socialist government. The Italian economy is too unruly and uncontrollable to be a significant force in the world economy. The discussion here will focus on West Germany, the United Kingdom and Japan.[7]

As recorded in Table I, West German inflation is enviably low and still falling, despite the adverse effects of the deutsche mark depreciation against the dollar and in lesser degree against the yen and the pound sterling. Since 1980 unemployment has more than doubled and is still rising. Job vacancies have virtually vanished. In the late 1970s, with unemployment at 3.5 to 4 percent, there were four unemployed for every vacancy. Now there are 40! Money-wage increases have slowed to 3.5 percent per year. After allowance for productivity trends, labor costs per unit of output are stable or declining. Could anyone seriously contend that macroeconomic expansion is now barred by rigidly high real wage rates? Surely at least half of current unemployment is Keynesian, not classical.

The view that West Germany was afflicted by classical unemployment, that its "natural rate" rose after 1973, gained currency during the post-OPEC stagflation. The onset of expensive energy coincided with immigration restrictions that limited the role of potential *Gastarbeiter* as an uncounted reserve army of unemployed. One signal of structural deterioration is that during the last ten years unemployment of labor rose more than underutilization of capacity. Another signal was the rise in the "wage gap," a

---

[7] The OECD *Economic Outlook* series and *Economic Surveys* of particular countries are indispensable sources. The Bruno-Sachs paper cited in footnote 3 and the Sachs paper cited in footnote 4 are very important in advancing the argument that supply limits and the "wage-gap" were the important constraints on output in OECD economies outside North America after OPEC I. However, in the second paper Sachs concludes that a large component of European unemployment in 1981 was Keynesian, and presumably an even larger proportion of 1983-84 unemployment is attributable to deficient demand. In a study for the Center for Economic Policy Studies of the European Community, R. Dornbusch, G. Basevi, O. Blanchard, W. Buiter, and R. Layard, "Macroeconomic Prospects and Policies for the European Community," Brussels, April 1983, argue the case for a coordinated expansion. See Wolfgang Franz, "German Unemployment and Stabilization Policy," *European Economic Review*, No. 21, 1983, for a careful econometric analysis leading to the conclusion that the German natural rate of unemployment is now around 4%, or 4.7%, according to an amendment by R. J. Gordon in the same issue.

measure of unit labor costs relative to prices, compared to a base year, specifically one of normal pre-OPEC prosperity, 1969. An increase in the wage gap is a squeeze on profit margins. The gap rose significantly, perhaps as much as 10 percent, in the early 1970s, but it has since declined to its 1969 norm. In any event, labor costs relative to after-tax net incomes to capital are low in West Germany compared to the United States. (In 1974 and 1982 the West German ratios were 3.1 and 3.0 respectively, while the American ratios were 3.6 and 3.4.) The wage-gap theory of the post-OPEC West German slowdown through 1979 is plausible, though debatable. It is not a credible explanation of the rise of unemployment in the 1980s.

The trend of potential real output in West Germany, i.e., output at a constant unemployment rate, is lower than before 1973, but still appears to exceed 3 percent per year. The bulk of it is productivity growth; the labor force is virtually stationary. A conservatively high estimate of the present inflation-safe rate of unemployment is 4.5 percent. The "Okun's law" coefficient, relating percentage shortfalls of real GDP to excess unemployment, seems to be 2 or 2.5. Thus the loss of GDP at 9.5 percent unemployment is 10 to 12 percent. Eliminating it would take five years of growth in real GDP averaging around 5 percent per year. With so much room and time, the Bundesbank and government would have plenty of chance to apply the brakes on evidence of price acceleration before unemployment fell the full amount.

There is another reason why fatalistic acceptance of the classical unemployment thesis is especially puzzling for West Germany. The history of wage determination in the Federal Republic is by and large not one of confrontation but one of moderation and "codetermination."[8] Realities of international competitiveness, macroeconomic trade-offs and monetary and fiscal policies have influenced collective bargaining more successfully than in most other countries, including the United States and the United Kingdom. This has been true even after 1977, when the unions withdrew from the annual summit sessions with representatives of em-

---

[8] R. J. Flanagan, D. W. Soskice and Lloyd Ulman, *Unionism, Economic Stabilization, and Income Policies: European Experience*, Washington D.C.: Brookings Institution, 1983, Chapter 5.

ployers, the central bank, the government, and the Council of Economic Experts. Rigidities are not built into the system. Contracts last only one year, and indexation is outlawed. Government, unions and employers have recognized that wage setting is a matter of national political economy and economic politics. The West German government has actively pursued incomes policies, using macroeconomic policies and the wage-employment trade-offs they imply as both threats and promises.

If, as the influential economist Herbert Giersch has argued,[9] West Germany needs a *Lohnpause* (pause in wage increases) to clear the road for macroeconomic expansion, the record does not suggest, at least to an outside observer, that it could not be negotiated in return for a promise that policy will assure the expansion. If, under its new conservative government, West Germany is in the process of reforming its system of labor relations in the direction of decentralization, nonintervention and confrontation, the outsider may be excused for observing "if it ain't broke, don't fix it."

The situation of the United Kingdom is similar to that of West Germany, except that unemployment and inflation are both about three points higher. Both wages and unit labor costs have been decelerating, while a modest recovery—enough to raise capacity utilization and employment but not to stop the unemployment rate from rising—has been under way for two years. Of course, labor relations and wage behavior have been throughout Great Britain's postwar history a much greater source of macroeconomic difficulty than in West Germany. Evidently a major objective of the Thatcher government has been to break the unions' grip on the economy. The question is whether, after five years of disinflationary policy and rising unemployment, the groundwork for expansion without wage and price acceleration is finally in place. And if not yet, when? Maybe by now even British trade union leaders would be ready to offer wage stability in exchange for jobs.

Japan absorbed the two OPEC shocks of the 1970s and the subsequent world slumps with remarkable success. Real growth was

---

[9] Cited and quoted in translation by Dornbusch *et al.*, *op. cit.*, in footnote 7. Giersch's article is "Kaufkraft und Lohne," from Deutsche Bundesbank, *Auszuge aus Presseartikeln*, November 6, 1982.

interrupted only mildly in 1974-75. But growth rates after OPEC I were less than half the double-digit annual rates common previously, and they fell still farther in the 1980s. These slowdowns have opened a wide GDP gap, suggested by declining indicators of capacity utilization but not easy to discern in unemployment statistics. The 1983 unemployment rate, though under 3 percent, is twice the rate of 1972. In Japan, far more than in Western economies, slack demand is absorbed by keeping redundant workers on the payroll—in effect a system of private unemployment insurance. As a result, the Okun coefficient for Japan is estimated to be from 13 to 25.[10] The lower number indicates that an extra point of unemployment in Japan signifies the same degree of slack as an extra five points in the United States or West Germany. Today, therefore, Japanese production is far below potential trend.

Like West Germany's, Japan's inflation is low and declining. With the help of a one-shot reduction of real wages, Japan overcame the inflationary consequences of the first oil shock by 1978. The second one Japan took pretty much in stride. Wage pressure is a minor problem in a country where unions are weak and the bonus system makes labor costs move up and down with employers' ability to pay—the workers' quid pro quo for immunity from layoffs.

IV. Demand Management Policies in the Major OECD Economies

The severe decline in world economic activity since 1979 was the result of restrictive macroeconomic policies deliberately and concurrently adopted in almost all major countries. The common goal was to overcome the price acceleration accompanying the second oil crisis, when oil demands enhanced by the 1975-79 recovery confronted supplies interrupted by the Iranian revolution and the beginnings of the Iran-Iraq war.

---

[10] Koichi Hamada and Yoshio Kurosaka, "The Relationship between Production and Unemployment in Japan: Okun's Law in Comparative Perspective," paper presented at International Seminar on Macroeconomics, Paris, Maison des Sciences de l'Homme, June 1983.

The firm, unanimous and single-minded dedication of macro policies to the conquest of inflation reflected experience after the first OPEC shock in 1973-74. Then too, restrictive policies brought severe recession and disinflation throughout the world. But subsequent experience differed from country to country. The most striking differences were between the United States and the two other big locomotives, West Germany and Japan. In the United States, fiscal and monetary policies turned stimulative or accommodative in 1975, and the subsequent recovery lowered unemployment rates by more than three percentage points. In West Germany and Japan, the macro brakes were relaxed very little. Unemployment and economic slack in those countries, indeed throughout the OECD outside North America, remained much higher than before. But the more austere governments preserved more of the disinflationary gains of the mid-decade recession and were less vulnerable to inflation following the second oil price shock. The United States and Canada, together with those European countries (notably the United Kingdom, France and Italy) with chronically high inflation, were also vulnerable to crises of confidence in foreign exchange markets. The lesson perceived by all central banks was applied as the second OPEC shock hit: tighten promptly, tighten hard and stay tight.

Disinflation, Depression and Recovery in the United States

In the United States, Federal Reserve Board Chairman Paul Volcker announced in October 1979 a policy of relentless gradual reductions in the growth rates of monetary aggregates to continue until monetary growth would accommodate only sustainable non-inflationary rates of increase in gross national product (GNP). The policy differed from the restrictive measures taken in mid-1974 by Chairman Arthur Burns and his Federal Reserve colleagues in Volcker's explicit disavowal of countercyclical monetary policy. This time the "Fed" would not rescue the economy from recession by accommodating continuing inflation, as the Burns regime was perceived to have done from 1975. In the United States, as in the United Kingdom and Europe, many economists, financiers and policymakers believed that the effectiveness of recession as therapy for inflation was diluted and rendered transitory by the expectations of workers, unions and businesses that anti-recessionary policies would save them from hard times whether or not they gave way on nominal wages and prices. The same theory predicted that if the private sector were convinced that policymakers would "stay the course," a disinflationary recession would be shorter and do less damage than past recessions to employment and production.[11] The theory has influenced fiscal as well as monetary policies in most major economies: the Thatcher and Reagan governments foreswear countercyclical macro policies as a matter of principle, and others act in the same spirit.

The Federal Reserve nevertheless relented in the late summer and fall of 1982. United States inflation rates had by then fallen dramatically. But the side effects, in unemployment, business failures, lost production and low investment, were much more damaging to the American and world economies than had been intended. The advertised commitment to "stay the course" had not noticeably speeded the disinflation or limited the damage. Third World debtor countries, notably Mexico and Brazil, could not earn enough hard currency in export markets to carry debts at the high interest rates resulting from restrictive monetary policies in the United States and elsewhere. Their difficulties threatened the solvency of their creditors in North America and Europe. A sharp decline in the velocity of money in the United States, partly because deregulation was making checking accounts in banks more attractive vehicles for saving and partly because general pessimism increased preference for safe, government-insured liquid assets, was making the Federal Reserve's money supply targets even more restrictive of nominal GNP than had been expected. When

---

[11] The theory is associated in the economics profession with the "new classical macroeconomics" and the "rational expectations" revolution. Independently the late William Fellner set forth the "credible threat" policy in several papers and in his book *Towards a Reconstruction of Macroeconomics*, Washington, D.C.: American Enterprise Institute, 1976. For exposition and criticism of these ideas see the papers of McCallum, Fellner, Tobin and Okun in *Journal of Money, Credit and Banking*, November 1980, part 2. For tests of the theory against the recent disinflationary recession, see papers by George Perry and by Fellner and Philip Cagan in *Brookings Papers on Economic Activity*, No. 2, Washington, D.C.: Brookings Institution, 1983.

those targets were suspended to allow higher money growth, interest rates of all maturities fell sharply, and interest-sensitive expenditures, for residential construction and consumer durable goods, revived. The economy turned up in November, assisted strongly by the usual cyclical rhythm of inventories as businesses stopped liquidating them and began re-stocking.

The strong recovery of final sales of goods and services (GNP less net inventory accumulation) throughout 1983 was powerfully assisted by consumers spending the proceeds of two 10-percent cuts of personal income tax rates, one in July 1982 and one in July 1983. These were the second and final installments of the three rate reductions scheduled in the Economic Recovery Tax Act of 1981. Likewise the buildup of defense spending, also planned in 1981, began to provide markets and jobs, more via the placement of orders than by actual outlays.

By pure serendipity the Administration carried out a classic well-timed Keynesian anti-recession fiscal policy complementary to the countercyclical change in monetary policy in late 1982. Neither of the deficit-increasing measures was intended to be a demand stimulus. In 1981 no recession clouded the officially projected scenario, and the Administration was on principle opposed to countercyclical demand management. The tax cuts were supply-side incentives, intended to encourage saving, work and risktaking, not spending. The defense buildup was for national security and diplomatic strategy, not for any economic purpose.

Whatever their motivations, expansionary monetary and fiscal policies worked as traditionally expected in the United States in 1983. Three or four million new jobs[12] were created, and the unemployment rate came down from 10.7 percent to 7.8 percent. As recently as the summer of 1982, the air was full of pessimism about the intractability of unemployment: the feeling then was that even as business activity recovers it will not create jobs. Congress, in a desperate attempt to do something, raised gasoline taxes

---

[12] The ambiguity arises from an unusual discrepancy between the gains in employment reported in the household survey by workers and those reported in the establishment survey by employers. The former is the higher number; possibly the reduction of unemployment, remarkably large considering the growth of output, is an overstatement.

to fund additional public jobs. The program was to create at most 300,000 jobs, but at least an equal number were probably lost by diversion of private spending to tax payment. Also as recently as early 1983 the air was full of dire predictions that federal deficits would "choke off recovery," even while pragmatic business forecasters correctly knew they would do the opposite.

The 1979-82 episode achieved a substantial but incomplete victory over inflation in the United States. The "core" inflation rate, which excludes patently nonrecurrent price changes, has fallen four or five points, from nine to ten percent per year to four to five percent per year. Wage inflation has fallen similarly; what this portends for price inflation depends on the productivity trend of the 1980s, which is not yet clear. In any event recovery has not reversed, or even arrested, gradual progress on inflation to date. This was to have been expected given the slack in utilization of labor and capacity still remaining. It was not to have been anticipated by those who expect price inflation to follow monetary growth regardless of the economic climate, because the Federal Reserve allowed double-digit growth of M-1 (currency in circulation plus demand deposits) from July 1982 to June 1983. (Since then M-1 growth has slowed to four percent, leading some monetarists to predict an early recession.)

The Federal Reserve has by no means abandoned its anti-inflation objective. After the initial drop of interest rates in 1982, the Federal Reserve raised them about 100 basis points in June 1983 and has held them steady to date. Paul Volcker and his colleagues will probably be content so long as, on the one side, no new recession begins and, on the other side, the expansion is well-behaved. A well-behaved recovery in this context means that the pace is slowing and approaching sustainable growth; prices and wages are not accelerating; unemployment is safely above the six percent rate of 1978-79; and monetary aggregates are within the target ranges for their growth, lower for 1984 than for 1983. In the absence of any one of those conditions, Chairman Volcker has made clear that the "Fed" is ready to apply the brakes and raise interest rates. Continued recovery will not receive the benefit of the doubt against the risk of accelerating inflation.

Interest rates in the United States are still by historical standards very high in relation to actual inflation and to reasonable expectations of future inflation. These rates are a formidable obstacle to accumulation of domestic capital—residential and non-residential, human and physical, private and public, fixed and working. They are even more devastating to United States foreign investment; here indeed the nation is disinvesting, running large deficits on current account because of enormous merchandise trade deficits. How long the sheer momentum of the recovery, the general optimistic mood and the fiscal stimulus can prevail over these obstacles is the main near-term uncertainty about the strength and duration of the recovery.

United States Interest Rates and the World Economy

The mechanisms by which American interest rates crowd out the nation's net exports is a striking illustration of textbook analysis of the workings of macroeconomic policies in today's international monetary environment, a world of floating exchange rates and closely connected financial markets. As differentially high interest rates have attracted funds into dollar-denominated assets, the dollar has appreciated against the yen, deutsche mark, franc and other currencies—actually by 52 percent on average since 1980, 45 percent when account is also taken of differences in national inflations over the period. The appreciation handicaps American exports and encourages imports.

The unique strength of United States recovery in 1983, and prospectively in 1984, also raises American imports while the sluggishness of foreign economies continues to depress their demands for American exports. Dollar appreciation since 1979 has, on the other hand, contributed to disinflation in the United States by making imported goods less expensive in dollars—U.S. inflation is estimated to be one or two percentage points lower as a result.[13] But this effect is only a transitory contribution to disinflation. It cannot be repeated without further appreciation, and it is more likely to be reversed.

While interest-rate differentials are the major source of the dollar's strength in exchange markets, they are not the only factor.

---

[13] Otto Eckstein, "Disinflation," *Data Resources Economic Studies Series*, No. 114, October 1983.

International political developments and longer run assessments of economic prospects may have improved the dollar's standing as a safe haven. There is no assurance that continued interest differentials will maintain the dollar's exchange value. Portfolio adjustments to exploit the perceived advantages of dollar assets in risk and return are not endless; most of them may have already occurred. United States' current-account deficits shift wealth to foreigners who tend to prefer their home currencies. Those deficits also raise doubts about the long-run viability of America's heavy reliance on foreign borrowing to finance its budget deficits and domestic investments.

High American interest rates and the high exchange value of the dollar have been and still are important determinants of the world macroeconomic environment in several respects. First, because of the weight of the United States in international financial markets, high interest rates in the United States make interest rates high everywhere. In this way they contributed to the universal world depression, and they are still an obstacle to world recovery. Second, they intensify Third World debt burdens, especially in a period of disinflation and depression. Third, the appreciation of the dollar has exacerbated trade frictions, particularly between the United States and Japan, and inspired protectionist measures and proposals in the United States. Fourth, American interest and exchange rates have constrained macroeconomic policy options in Europe and Japan, although not as tightly as those governments claim. This point will be discussed in the next section.

Monetary and Fiscal Policies Outside North America

The 1983 recovery was unique to North America, and so were the shifts to expansionary macroeconomic policies. Europe and Japan lag far behind, benefiting from the spillover of American demand into their economies but doing nothing else to stimulate domestic demand. Their certainties that active policies of expansion would be futile and inflationary should be reconsidered in light of the American example.

As stated above, monetary policies in those other countries are in some degree constrained by American interest rates. Major foreign central banks have lost some control of their own interest rates and exchange rate, but not all. The more expansionary their domestic monetary policy is, the lower their own interest rates will be, and the more their exchange rates will depreciate. Such depreciation is advantageous to exports and to domestic economic activity and employment. In effect, foreign central banks could capture for their own economies even more of the expansion of demand in North America than they already have. In particular, this is a realistic opportunity for Great Britain, whose international competitive position is still less favorable than in the 1970s.

There are several reasons they do not exploit this opportunity. It would raise the local prices of imports invoiced in dollars, not just goods of American origin but other internationally traded goods, notably oil. Inflation statistics would be temporarily worsened. Moreover, central banks impose on themselves monetarist targets and are determined to stick by them. A special reason applies to Japan, the fear of increased trade friction with the United States.

What about fiscal policy in the major economies outside North America? Demand stimulus by tax reductions or government spending would not lower interest rates and further depreciate currencies against the dollar but would have the reverse effects. Those effects, indeed, would create room for additional monetary expansion at existing interest and exchange rates, if monetary targets were adjusted accommodatively. In fact, however, fiscal policies outside North America are severely restrictive, not stimulative. All major governments are trying to reduce their budget deficits by fiscal economies and tax increases.

The depression itself has, of course, automatically increased actual budget deficits, both by drastically reducing revenues and by requiring increased outlays for unemployment compensation and for relief of economic distress. Those features of modern fiscal systems, which raise deficits in cyclical recessions and lower them in recoveries and prosperities, are "built-in stabilizers." They sustain incomes and spending during downturns and restrict them in booms. Cyclical deficits are passive consequences of bad times. They buffer the decline in demand but do not actively stimulate demand.

Measures to overcome cyclical deficits are actively contractionary, intensifying recession or retarding recovery. This lesson was supposedly learned long ago, for example in the early 1930s from the counterproductive efforts of Presidents Herbert Hoover and Franklin D. Roosevelt to balance the U.S. federal budget and from the disastrous consequences of Chancellor Bruning's sacrifice of German unemployed to fiscal orthodoxy. The fiscal policies of major European governments and Japan in the 1980s are similarly perverse, if less extreme.

Table II summarizes the effects on budget deficits of recent fiscal actions in the seven summit economies and the OECD as a whole, and compares them with the passive cyclical components of recent deficits. The Table shows remarkable "success" in wiping out the built-in stabilizers. Another way to interpret these policies is to consider their effects on the "structural" or "high employment" budget deficits, i.e., those that would hypothetically occur if economic activity were on its normal growth trend. Those deficits are being significantly reduced, in some countries transformed into surpluses. The Thatcher government, for a notable example, has moved the budget into substantial structural surplus, a remarkable "achievement" during a long and severe economic decline. Evidently the general objective is to raise the unemployment rate and lower the GDP level at which permanently acceptable budget outcomes will be achieved. In other words, these governments have lowered their sights and are adapting their budgets to macroeconomic performance chronically weaker than in the past.

TABLE II   Fiscal Policies and Outcomes in Major OECD Economies

	(a) Increases in surplus (decreases in deficit), % of GNP or GDP, cumulative 1981-1984			(b) Budget deficits relative to GNP/GDP, and to net private saving (%)	
	Actual	Cyclical	Noncyclical	1983	1984
United States	−2.5	−0.9	−1.6	3.8, 67.8	3.7, 58.3
Japan	+2.0	−0.9	+2.9	3.4, 28.3	2.5, 22.2
West Germany	+1.0	−3.7	+4.7	3.1, 37.3	2.1, 26.1
France	−4.1	−3.8	−0.3	3.4, 47.0	3.8, 52.9
United Kingdom	+1.2	−3.4	+4.6	2.7, 54.8	2.3, 46.1
Seven summit countries	−1.4	−2.0	+0.6	4.1, 56.1	3.8, 48.4

Notes: OECD calculations and estimates for 1983 and 1984. Figures cover both subordinate and central governments.
(a) The figures shown are sums of four annual figures. This approximation is not strictly accurate but is indicative. Noncyclical changes are discretionary actions on taxes and outlays. Cyclical changes are passive responses to economic fluctuations, given the tax legislation and the budget program. Actual changes are the sum of the two.

Source: Economic Outlook, OECD, December 1983, Tables 9, 10 and 13.

Almost all of these countries have higher national propensities to save than the United States. Even in prosperous times, when private investment demands are strong, they have less reason to worry about the "crowding out" consequences of government deficits. In these slack times, their saving is ample to finance both public and private borrowers, and indeed to acquire dollar claims as well. Table II also shows deficits in various economies relative to national saving.

The tightening of fiscal policies in the locomotive economies of Europe and Japan has serious international ramifications. Fiscal stimulus would not only increase domestic demands and employment but raise imports, spilling badly needed demand into the rest of the world—the smaller countries of Europe and Asia, the Third World in general and North America. By putting their fiscal engines into perverse gear, Europe and Japan are setting back recovery throughout the world.

Appropriately stimulative policies need not, by the way, commit any country to high budget deficits in times of prosperity because tax cuts or job-creating expenditures could be designed to terminate at a scheduled date or contingent on economic circumstances. They need not favor consumption, public or private; they could take the form of tax incentives for investment or of public investment projects. They need not commit governments to larger public sectors than they desire in the long run. Whatever the national priorities of the country and its social philosophy with respect to the roles of public and private economic activity, they can be reconciled with fiscal policies appropriate to macroeconomic circumstances.

The contrast in macroeconomic policies between the United States and the other locomotives of the world economy is striking. The United States is pursuing a tight high-interest monetary policy, albeit one that was sufficiently relaxed a year and a half ago to avert economic and financial collapse and start recovery. American fiscal policy is easy and becoming looser every fiscal year. The combination has produced a vigorous recovery at home and arrested economic decline throughout the world. But the extreme policy mix portends serious problems for the United States in the future, and the contagious high interest rates retard recovery elsewhere. Other countries have a right to complain, though they should address their complaints to American monetary authorities as well as the fiscal policymakers in the White House and the Congress. With unchanged monetary policy, tightening of the U.S. budget would worsen, not relieve, the economic predicaments of other nations. Europe and Japan, in contrast, are pursuing tight monetary and tight fiscal policies both. Their monetary policies are tight because of U.S. interest rates and their own monetarist principles. Their fiscal policies are, for the most part, difficult to understand and justify.

Both West Germany and Japan have traditionally enjoyed and depended on export-driven growth of demand and have eschewed demand management for either domestic or international objectives. Both governments have plenty of room for expansionary fiscal policy and have high-saving citizens to whom to sell bonds. The continued series of budget austerities of these governments seem quite misguided. Both countries have domestic needs, individual and collective, to which their unused potential product could be devoted. Both could expand their assistance to the less developed countries. It is high time for these reluctant locomotives to pull their shares of the weight of the world economic train.

Macroeconomic expansion is the key to progress against unemployment. It will not solve all the problems, to be sure. The pathology of urban neighborhoods that condemns nearly half of black youth to unemployment cannot be cured by monetary and fiscal policy. The same is true of growing youth unemployment in Europe. Macro policies and general prosperity will not restore the old high-wage jobs in smokestack industries in the American Midwest or the Ruhr. There is plenty of room and need for intelligent public policies to treat these difficult cases. But they will be hopeless unless general prosperity and growth are restored. That is the first and highest priority.

V. International Coordination of Macroeconomic Policies: The Challenge to the Leaders of the Summit Economies

From an international standpoint, policy corrections are needed both in the United States and in the other locomotives of the world economy. These require international cooperation. Monetary stimulus by any single country acting alone expands home demand and at the same time depreciates its currency to the benefit of its exports and to the detriment of its trading partners. Internationally concerted monetary stimulus that lower interest rates simultaneously everywhere can give the whole world economy a boost, expanding everybody's exports and imports and creating no trade imbalances. The United States is in the position to take the lead. Since our interest and exchange rates are too high, other countries could lower interest rates by smaller amounts, narrowing the differential and engineering an orderly decline in the exchange value of the dollar. Continuing on the present course may at any time provoke a disorderly decline of the dollar.

In fiscal policy, the United States would be shifting to a tighter budget while other countries would substitute for their fiscal restrictions expansionary measures appropriate to the economic situations in their own economies and in the world at large. These monetary and fiscal actions should be the major agenda of the next economic summit conference; no topics deserve higher priority.

Can the major economic powers effectively coordinate their macroeconomic policies? On the record, the prospects are not good. It is true that central banks agreed, after the second oil shock, on single-minded disinflationary policy. The heads of the seven economic summit governments affirmed the priority at their Venice and Ottawa meetings in 1980 and 1981 respectively. Since that was the disposition of each country individually, agreement and synchronization were not difficult to achieve. At Williamsburg in 1983 unemployment and stagnation were clearly the pressing macroeconomic problems of the day. The best the group could do was to commit their governments to attack their structural budget deficits. Fortunately, President Reagan, the target of this vote, did not take it seriously. Unfortunately, his peers did.

The nine annual economic summits[14] have usually concentrated on energy, trade and commerce with the Soviet bloc. At the Bonn summit of 1978, however, the United States succeeded—in return for pledging decontrol of its domestic oil prices, a long overdue

---

[14] For a useful review of economic summitry, see George de Menil and Anthony M. Solomon, *Economic Summitry*, New York: Council on Foreign Relations, Inc., pp. 30-34 and 78-79.

reform—in persuading reluctant allies to fire up their locomotives. Several governments promised increased growth of output. West Germany and France agreed to specific amounts of extra fiscal stimulus, 1 percent and 0.5 percent respectively. Japan and the United Kingdom had already instituted expansionary budget measures—Japan in response to American diplomatic pressure prior to the summit. The United States, whose recovery had been running ahead of the others, promised modest fiscal contractions. Six months later the Shah of Iran was overthrown. The world was hit by the second oil shock, a new spurt of inflation and international financial disarray. The locomotive theory of the Carter Administration was discredited, along with demand management in general. That legacy stands in the way of any internationally coordinated recovery program, even though the locomotive theory seems quite correct in today's circumstances.

Perhaps our leaders could be inspired by an earlier example. As the decade of the 1960s began, the world economy had been beset by a slump, by an unpleasant history of inflation and by international monetary disturbances. The United States had suffered two recessions in quick succession, designed to bring down an unacceptably high inflation rate and to protect the dollar. As recovery from the slump began, the Ministerial Council of the OECD announced that the member nations (which did not yet include Japan) had pledged themselves to aim for a 50 percent growth of output by the end of the decade for the group as a whole. The Council noted that this growth would not only increase the welfare and strength of the member countries but would lead to an increased flow of resources to developing countries.[15] Though this declaration was a statement of hope and intent, it was taken seriously by member governments both individually and in their consultations with each other on specific macroeconomic issues. In the event, the growth target was fulfilled with room to spare.

The present situation is more serious and more difficult. It will take statesmanship and imaginative leadership to turn the 1980s from a decade of unemployment and stagnation to one of prosperity and progress, from a period of discord in the alliance over

---

[15] Reported in *Economic Report of the President*, 1962, Washington D.C.: U.S. Government Printing Office, 1962, p. 38.

competition and trade to one of cooperation and mutual benefit. Alliances are strengthened not just by resolving conflicts of interest but by undertaking together enterprises that offer substantial benefits to all. Macroeconomic policy coordination is a good place to begin.

I am greatly indebted to Gabriel de Kock for his capable research assistance and instruction, but the opinions and errors are my own responsibility. I have benefited greatly from the expertise of Sylvia Ostry, both from personal conversation and from her article, "The World Economy: Marking Time," Foreign Affairs, *America and the World, 1983.*

Shirley Williams

Unemployment and Economic Strains in the Western Alliance

On January 21, 1984, *The Economist* produced a cover showing a debonair, but old-fashioned, cartoon European. This composite figure purported to show how Americans see Europeans: snooty, mean, quarrelsome and cowardly. A similar composite could be created to reflect the European view of Americans and would most likely portray a macho, gun-slinging, cowboy figure, convinced of his righteousness and insensitive to his neighbors. Both figures reveal more about U.S.-West European relations, which are seriously strained at the moment, than they do about either Americans or Europeans per se. Ironically, this tension exists despite an unusual coincidence of political views—for with the exception of France and Canada, all the larger countries of the Atlantic Alliance are governed by conservatives, and most of these governments are pursuing cautious, orthodox economic policies.

The strains in the Alliance have several sources: one is defense. Carrying out the missile deployment portion of the 1979 dual-track decision has cost European governments in the Alliance a good deal in terms of popularity with their publics and has marked the end of the political consensus on Western defense that was previously embraced by almost all European political parties, from conservatives to socialists. Another source of strain lies in differing European and American perceptions of the Soviet bloc and in disagreements about what are the best methods for contending with communist ideology.

I. Economic Strains

In this essay, however, I will concentrate on a less-often debated area, that of economic policy. To some extent economic strains within the Western Alliance are inevitable. After all, the European Economic Community (EEC) and the United States compete with one another in third markets. Both have "smokestack" industries that are suffering due to a lack of adequate demand for their products, and both are cognizant of the possibility of "dumping," or selling goods below cost. This inevitable competition is aggravated by the partial exclusion of the United States from a traditional market for agricultural products—Western Europe. It is exacerbated by the EEC's subsidization of European agricultural surpluses sold to third markets. There is no doubt that the United States has a genuine and powerful grievance vis-à-vis the operation of the Common Agricultural Policy (CAP) in this respect.

The EEC has its own grievances with the United States. One of these regards the operation of the COCOM (Coordinating Committee for Export Controls) rules, which regulate exports of technologically advanced products to the Soviet bloc. Exports of computer-related products are becoming more and more important economically. European electronics firms. believe the COCOM rules are sometimes misused to exclude them from markets in the Soviet bloc and China and to hinder them in competing with U.S. companies—not to protect Western technological inventions of potential strategic value.

Compounding these strains within the Alliance is current U.S. economic policy, which combines monetary stringency with fiscal profligacy and thus produces, as we all know, exceptionally high real interest rates and a strong dollar. That strong dollar is making the U.S. manufacturing industry uncompetitive, and worsening the American balance of trade with the outside world. It is estimated by Data Resources, a U.S.-based economic information service, which undertook a study recently on behalf of nine U.S. blue-chip multinational companies, that there would have been a million more jobs in the United States if the dollar had remained at its 1980 parity and that the U.S. balance of trade would have benefited to the tune of $25 billion.[1] Japanese imports into the United States continue to rise rapidly except where they are limited by mutual agreement as is the case with cars. The fear among Europeans is that the Administration will continue its present policies

---

[1] *The Financial Times*, February 1, 1984.

until the presidential election is over, since tax increases are very unpopular with the voters and since social expenditure cuts are unpopular with Congress. This would mean no reduction in projected budget deficits in 1985 and possibly not in 1986 either, even though in the Budget Message he issued to Congress in February 1984, President Ronald Reagan admitted that deficits on such a scale raised "the specter of sharply higher interest rates, choked-off investment, renewed recession and rising unemployment."[2] Such alarm bells toll even more loudly in Western Europe, where investment is low, recovery is weak, and unemployment has not declined at all from levels above those in the United States.

Western Economic Recovery and the Threats to It

The industrial world has been slowly climbing out of the longest recession since the Second World War. After two years of decline—fashionably known as negative growth—the gross national product (GNP) of the Organization of Economic Cooperation and Development (OECD) countries rose in 1983. The growth was outstanding (over five percent) in only three countries: the United States, Japan and Canada, the first of which embarked upon the classically Keynesian fiscal policy for correcting a recession—big budget deficits and substantial tax cuts. This policy has led to a satisfactorily Keynesian conclusion: U.S. industrial production and GNP grew in 1983 like the proverbial green bay tree.

More than that, the growth was sufficient to absorb modest increases in labor productivity and to create new jobs. Unemployment in the United States fell by 2.5 million, and 4 million new jobs were created. But the question that haunts Europe is whether the American economic recovery can continue.

Western Europe's much more modest economic recovery, fueled almost entirely by a mild consumer boom, which was financed partly by higher earnings and partly by dissaving, has not so far reduced unemployment. Indeed, unemployment has edged up in every single European country, though the rapid upsurge of the 1979 to 1982 period has leveled out. Industrial productivity, partly because so many weaker firms went out of business and so

---

2 *The New York Times*, February 2, 1984, p. 1.

much labor was shed, increased quite quickly from 1979 to 1982. There is no longer a large stock of underused labor in Europe, but firms are still working well below capacity, and capital equipment is underused. It would require a sustained upturn in demand for industrial firms to take on many new workers.

In their present mood of fiscal and monetary stringency (though there has been a slight relaxation in the United Kingdom recently), European governments are reluctant to act as locomotives for the next round of economic growth. Given their budgetary positions and low public sector borrowing, however, there is a strong argument for West Germany and the United Kingdom to do so. But both are transfixed by the evidence that inflation is edging up again and that wages, despite the efforts of ministers and employers to push them down, are proving very difficult to manage.

That leaves Japan, with its booming balance-of-payments surplus ($21 billion in 1983), its rising exports (plus 5.8 percent) and its falling imports (minus 4.1 percent), its 2.5 percent unemployment, and its under 2 percent inflation. But Japan is unlikely to act as the locomotive to keep the recovery going. While Japan exports some capital to Western Europe and the United States, its investment funds do not wash across the world looking for the highest interest rates. One of the remarkable facts about Japan is that internal investment was sustained during the world recession at interest rates far below those on offer in New York or London or Frankfurt. Even today, real interest rates in Japan are little over half those in the main Western industrial countries—3.5 percent versus 6.5 percent. Japan is part of, yet partly separate from, the increasingly interdependent world economy. It is heavily dependent on trade, though proportionately less so than the United Kingdom, but it is culturally still so distinct that economic pressures can lead to different results than would be the case anywhere else. For instance, tight labor markets have created none of the inflationary pressures in Japan that are associated with them in the West.

So the question of how long the recovery can be sustained comes back to the United States, and the answers are to be found in politics, not in economics. High interest rates have attracted enough capital from the rest of the world to finance the U.S. budget deficit, running at about $180 to $200 billion a year for the next four years. Americans feel little affected personally since, unlike most Europeans, they can write off interest payments against taxes. Meanwhile the tax cuts and the rapidly increasing defense budget, for which the Reagan Administration has requested a whopping 14 percent boost this year, create jobs and keep money ringing merrily in the nation's tills. What president seeking reelection would want to change all that?

The American Role

Yet the inevitable repercussions darken the economic sky. For the United States is, like the rest of us, not an island but, to use John Donne's words, "part of the main." In a world economy where interdependence has risen by leaps and bounds, where trade has increased three times as fast as output, and where capital movements dwarf trade, the United States, the most important single economic power, has immense influence for good or ill on its neighbors and allies. Everyone recognizes that political expediency dictates that there will be neither tax increases nor cuts in the U.S. defense budget before the 1984 election, although some hopes of the latter are being entertained because the President may wish to appear less hawkish. Economic common sense of course dictates otherwise. But economic common sense must take second place to American politics and the world must rely on the Federal Reserve Bank to hold the monetary dike against inflation. The Western world is accustomed to dancing to the tune of the U.S. electoral cycle. However, as *The Economist* observed acidly at the end of 1983, "At their worst, America's policy-makers are as parochial as Albania's."[3]

So it is assumed that, give or take one or two percent, interest rates will stay high, despite Europe's ardent desire to see them fall. It is assumed that the dollar will stay high, making U.S. goods less and less competitive abroad and driving up the already huge $65 billion U.S. trade deficit. American costs are estimated to be 28 percent less competitive than in 1979, even though U.S. wages have not risen. The effect on industries producing internationally traded goods, except in those like defense where the United States is dominant, is that the United States is losing some market share.

---

[3] "The Overblown Dollar," *The Economist*, December 17, 1983, p. 9.

Before I follow through the possible repercussions on pressures for protectionism, let me for a moment look at the other consequences of U.S. economic policies on Europe. I have referred to European concern about high U.S. interest rates, which both compels the Europeans to keep their own rates higher than they would wish (industrial investment is low and flat in Europe and has been for several years) and attracts needed capital across the Atlantic. The OECD has described European unemployment as "capital deficient unemployment." I do not agree with this argument in all particulars, but certainly capital is not flowing fast enough into new technologies, new research and development, and new skills in Europe to build a competitive basis for the future.

The consequences of U.S. policy are even more severe for the developing countries. Both oil contracts and debts are largely denominated in dollars. Poor countries, which have suffered from the consequences of the recession on their export revenues, now have to find more money to pay debt interest and repayments. To add to their burden, the entire decline in world oil prices has been offset for those countries that pay for their oil in dollars. There is little these countries can do: they are locked into their past debts, though rescheduling eases the burden a bit. In addition, much of their agriculture is now harnessed to high fertilizer use, irrigation and tractors—Western methods much more energy-dependent than traditional agriculture. The American refusal to pay more than $750 million a year to the International Development Association (IDA), the World Bank subsidiary that lends to the poorest countries of all, must have seemed like the sharpest of ironies.

Pressures for Protectionism

Returning to the possible repercussions of present U.S. economic policies on free trade, it seems they could damage the United States itself, causing job losses and market losses in traditional export industries by pricing the United States out of the world market, just as the British manufacturing industry was forced out of its markets between 1979 and 1981. A continuing high rate for the dollar will most affect the smokestack industries that make standard mass-produced goods where price is the critical selling factor. These are the industries—textiles, carpets, cars, household durables, and steel—already most under pressure and most ready to demand protection to save jobs. The temptation to buy votes by promising protection to save jobs peaks at the time of a presidential election. The U.S. Congress has some 65 measures, large and small, lined up to protect American industry, including the pending controversial domestic content bill. This would require any manufacturer selling more than 100,000 cars in the United States to use a specified percentage of American parts and labor, up to 90 percent. In addition, almost all the Democratic presidential candidates favor some protective legislation.

In two areas, the storm has already broken. The United States and the EEC countries are not very significant trading partners: indeed, U.S.-EEC trade is only about five percent of the world's total. But it is very important for certain industries, notably agriculture, chemicals and steel. Steel is a disaster area on both sides of the Atlantic—the result of recession, substitution of steel by other materials like alloys and plastics, and the loss of trade to the newly industrializing countries. The American and European steel manufacturers wrangle miserably over the shrinking market like dogs over a bone. The United States has now slapped a tariff on European specialty steel, which it claims is being sold below cost. The EEC has retaliated by putting additional tariffs on chemicals and sports equipment. All of this is fairly minor skirmishing; indeed, one might argue that the Western consensus on free, or at least fairly free, trade has held up remarkably well through the recession, and that the OECD countries have kept the spirit of the free trade pledge they made in 1977. But when EEC-U.S. trade squabbles surface in agriculture, the problem becomes much more serious.

The Common Argicultural Policy of the EEC is in part protectionist, and expensive. It provides an elaborate range of threshold and intervention prices that ensure that farmers produce far more grain, dairy products, wine and vegetables than European consumers can absorb. The CAP also guarantees that 70 percent of the EEC budget is spent on agriculture, some of it to subsidize European exports in third markets against competition from Europe's friends. Yet the central strategy of the CAP is correct: to sustain a healthy, efficient European agriculture so that Europe's consumers do not need to depend on imports of items produced in a temperate climate. In a hungry world, it is right to be a producer, not an importer, of the world's scarce food grains. Further, the CAP is a vital bonding force for the EEC, the sole fully integrated policy apart from the customs union itself. The trouble is that the policy has been too successful in keeping farm families on the land and in keeping many very small farms running. In the multiparty politics of Western Europe, well-organized interest groups (and none are better organized or tougher than the farmers) wield a lot of power. The European Commission's proposal for a freeze on farm prices in 1984 followed a year that saw farm incomes drop over 6 percent on average and as much as 21 percent in the Federal Republic of Germany, has been greeted with cries of anguish.

It will be difficult to get governments to agree. Yet without an agreement, expenditure will exceed resources, and national governments may have to bale out the $14.1 billion EEC farm budget when it runs out by paying national subsidies, nationally financed. France, for one, is seeking outside markets for grain, and has sold 1.3 million tons of wheat to the Soviet Union. Meanwhile worried bureaucrats wonder if they can limit imports of U.S. soya (worth $4 billion a year) or feedstuffs ($750 million) that undersell domestic alternatives. Any such action would be highly inflammatory in the current sensitive state of U.S.-EEC trade relations. It is of course fair to add that U.S. agriculture is itself heavily subsidized.

Another area, and one of growing significance, is inflamed already. The scars of the U.S. intervention in the trans-Siberian pipeline deal are still plain to see. It was not so much the U.S. desire to use sanctions as a means of expressing Western anger over the suppression of Solidarity in Poland that riled Europeans; indeed many could understand the sanctions argument even though the moral case was weakened by the U.S. resumption of grain sales to the Soviet Union. It was the American attempt to override domestic legislation governing U.S. subsidiaries in Europe that upset so many Europeans. That issue has surfaced again in the area of electronics. At the same time, COCOM's approach to microcomputers (personal computers) is in a hopeless muddle and has not been revised since 1978. The U.S. Department of Defense is proposing that microcomputer sales to the Soviet bloc be banned. International Computers Limited and other such British companies claim they sometimes wait months or years for clearance from COCOM, only to discover their potential customers have been supplied by American companies. The belief that COCOM is used as an instrument to delay and confuse European competitors in high-tech fields is very strong. Now Japan is coming on the scene and has unilaterally set a very short copyright period for software. This is advantageous to Japan since its computer systems depend on outside software designers.

High Technology and New Jobs

The world of high technology could become a new quagmire for U.S.-West European and Western-Japanese trade relations. Data networks are already being established by multinationals, especially those in banking and finance. Multinational corporations are the most important customers of information technology, as 80 percent of this technology is now sold to business purchasers. Access to multinational data banks will be vital to high-tech companies, who will seek the best value for their money regardless of national barriers. We live in an interdependent world; we are entering one where borders will be simply irrelevant.

Let me offer just one example. The chairman of Electricité de France said last year that there might eventually be only three or four telecommunications systems in the free world. That means possibly one for Europe, two for North America, and one for Japan. Such integration raises huge questions about national sovereignty, national security, and national culture. It offers Europe the choice of having one system, or perhaps none at all.

In the scramble to seize commanding heights in the new technolgies, strains will become acute. Already the tensions between U.S. multinationals and their European subsidiaries are considerable: When should a company obey U.S. law and when should it obey the law of the host country if the laws conflict? European Economic Community directives on information (the Vredeling proposals) and on industrial democracy (the EEC Fifth Directive) apply to European subsidiaries of U.S. multinationals, but no similar rules apply to the parent companies under U.S. law. The more the EEC flexes its muscles and produces integrated policies, the greater the potential for conflict with the United States.

Yet the EEC must achieve a further degree of internal integration if it is to survive at all. The early years were easy, because they coincided with the steady growth in trade and output and the low unemployment of the 1960s. As the late John F. Kennedy said, "a rising tide lifts all boats." But the troubled 1970s were much harsher for the Community and coincided with its expansion to include three members in economic difficulty—the United Kingdom, Ireland and Denmark. As the oil shocks, inflation, and then recession swept over the EEC, it clung to the achievement of the customs union, which was far from perfect (as tests for health, safety, consumer standards, etc. indicated), but which was operating and effective.

Now, however, if the EEC fails to develop an industrial policy, it will be overwhelmed by the scale of operations required by some of the new technologies. Aerospace, telecommunications, car and chemical manufacture, and oil refining need international, not merely national, markets. These are the big battalions; small firms may have a role as suppliers, but they cannot market or service the final products. Europe has to create European multinationals on a scale adequate to compete with American and Japanese multinationals, or else abdicate from the world market. There are enough—just enough—good firms, and there is enough—just enough—advanced research and development in telecommunications, electronics, biotechnology and new materials to sustain an effective European competitor. Very late in the day, European governments are trying to agree on common standards for telecommunications and information technology. European controlled multinationals, possibly combining publicly and privately owned companies, are essential to the development of the EEC.

On the other hand, only political power at the Community level can hope to regulate multinationals, for individual European governments can be traded off one against the other. The thought was aptly expressed by Andrew Shonfield in his posthumous book, *In Defence of the Mixed Economy*, edited by his wife Zuzanna: "Public power can only reassert itself, say, over the international capital market, by the surrender of sovereign national power." The EEC, Shonfield went on to argue, should be seen as " 'a joint-interest group'—an important experiment in bringing the new footloose 'barons' of international business under control."[4]

For the employment issue, the point is clear. The West has largely succeeded in resisting large scale protectionism with some

---

[4] *In Defence of the Mixed Economy*, Oxford: Oxford University Press, 1984, p. 172.

important exceptions such as restrictions on steel, autos, video equipment, and agriculture. Yet persistent, undented unemployment levels in Western Europe will make it harder to resist further protectionism, as will the effects of an expensive dollar on traditional smokestack industries. Since no one expects many new jobs in the smokestack industries, hope lies in services, and especially in services based on the new technologies. Hence the ability to adopt them quickly becomes crucial. The choice, as one commentator put it, may be new jobs or no jobs.

The United States is well placed to move technology up-market. The American electronics industry is growing fast and so are other new technolgies like lasers and biotechnology. The same is true of Japan. The loser is likely to be Western Europe, whose culture, academically oriented educational system, and often antagonistic industrial relations are less well adapted to meet the new technological challenges. West European economies are more rigidly and more centrally organized than that of the United States. A single company, or at most two or three, may dominate a whole sector of industry. The large banks are closely involved with the great national corporations. Antitrust and competition legislation is weak, and in parts of the market prices are controlled by governments or by large suppliers themselves. Although class structures are weakening, large corporations face large unions across a gulf of mutual suspicions. Yet neither the mutual antagonism nor traditional occupational structures are relevant to the new technolgies, which require innovation, independence, quality consciousness, and management-labor cooperation. The United States was never as dominated and distorted by industrialization as Western Europe. Much of America's pioneering and enterprising spirit survived, and the United States was large enough for different regions to develop in different ways. If the United States consisted only of Michigan, Pennsylvania and Ohio, it would resemble industrial northwest Europe. American structural problems, its legacy of traditional skills and attitudes, and the duration and level of its unemployment would then be much the same.

But there are signs of hope. Europe has been vigorous in disseminating knowledge of microelectronics. Computers have been installed in almost every British primary school. Thousands of French homes have been given free terminals linked to interactive systems as a demonstration project in telematics. West Germany will have cabled half its homes by 1986 and Great Britain has more fiber optics as a proportion of her telephone lines than any other country in the world. Courses in microelectronics for small firms, unemployed youngsters, managers and apprentices are proliferating. But the complicated differences between national standards and regulations are major handicaps. If they are compounded by U.S. laws that hamper European technical development, the strains on the Alliance could be great indeed. It is time the OECD and GATT (General Agreement on Tariffs and Trade) discussed, as French President François Mitterrand requested in 1982, the question of technology transfers, and drew up, as he proposed, some rules for dealing with technology. As for COCOM, it is absurd to revise computer lists once every ten years; as *The Economist* has pointed out, microcomputers being introduced in the United States this year will have the capacity of mainframe computers ten years ago.[5] But it is equally absurd to ban exports of personal microcomputers because they are at the forefront of computer technology; insofar as they are, the Russians can easily obtain all they need anyway.

High unemployment—whether general as in most of Europe, or more localized, as in the United States—will assuredly lead to a political backlash in favor of protectionism unless it is tackled in other ways. Before turning to those other ways, let me describe, in the next section, the nature of unemployment in contemporary Europe, and how it differs from unemployment in the United States.

II. Employment in the United States and Western Europe

Similarities and Differences

During the Second World War governments of the Western Allies came to accept full employment as one of their primary objectives. The 1944 White Paper in Great Britain specifically committed the

---

[5] "The Electronic Tide," *The Economist*, January 21, 1984, p. 17.

coalition government to that end. The Truman Administration in 1946 recognized full employment as a goal of domestic policy. Western governments were successful in achieving very high levels of employment in the 1950s and 1960s. In Western Europe unemployment averaged about three percent a year and rarely exceeded five percent right through to the first oil price shock in 1973. North American rates were somewhat higher, between four and six percent, but this was attributed to a higher level of frictional unemployment as people moved from job to job. High employment was accompanied by growth in per capita output, higher real wages, education extended in time and expanded in scope, and much better provision for pensions and health, especially in EEC Europe where basic pensions and a health service free, or nearly free, at time of need, covered most of the population. Typically, per capita income doubled or trebled in the generation after the war, between 1948 and 1973.

But during the same generation inflation took root. It was fed from several sources. In EEC Europe powerful unions in labor markets characterized by demand pressures drove wage rates well above productivity increases. Money wages rose on average 9 percent a year in France and Great Britain, and 11 percent a year in Italy between 1963 and 1973. Production failed to keep pace and unit labor costs went up roughly twice as fast as in the United States and Canada.

The United States contributed to inflation in other ways. President Lyndon B. Johnson's decision to finance the war in Vietnam by printing dollars and selling them in Europe (the so-called Eurodollars) rather than by cutting back on other areas of expenditure, created a major potential for inflation. The oil price leap of 1973 completed the picture. In the 1970s unemployment and inflation in the OECD countries were, roughly, twice as high as in the 1960s, while growth was less than half that of the 1960s.

OECD governments produced a range of responses to cope with the new economic situation that confronted them. The United States, faced with over eight percent unemployment after the sudden but short-lived 1974-75 recession, adopted public works and Comprehensive Training and Employment Act programs, which brought unemployment down to a more acceptable six percent by the end of the Carter Administration. The Europeans were more concerned about inflation: West Germany, despite its relatively low level of inflation, feared that it would be destabilizing. The British and Italians saw confidence in their currencies disappear as annual inflation moved into the high teens and twenties. Two policies vied for favor: income policies, based on voluntary restraint by trade union bargainers (West Germany, Sweden, Austria, and from 1976 to 1979, the United Kingdom); or control over the money supply, including cash limits on public expenditure, which in crude terms meant choosing between higher wages or more jobs. Unemployment, according to this second option, would no longer be avoided at all costs. It became a means of weakening union power and thereby reducing wage-push pressures.

Expectations play a significant role in inflationary pressure. The recession has been deeper and more sustained than was predicted when policies of restraint were adopted in the late 1970s and early 1980s; unemployment has risen to unprecedented heights, and manufacturing output has been running at a quarter to a third below capacity. It is argued by many liberal economists in Europe that inadequate demand is now the main cause of Europe's low growth and low investment but that (as the French experience in 1982 showed) no medium-sized country would dare reflate on its own. Hence the argument advanced in France and elsewhere that only a growth, employment and technology policy coordinated among OECD governments, or at the very least, among EEC ones, will allow some reflation without capital flight or serious consequences for national currencies.

Demography. In every OECD country birth rates soared from the mid-1950s to the mid-1960s and then fell almost as precipitately in the 1970s. In West Germany, for instance, births rose 800,000 in 1953 to over 1,050,000 in 1962 and then declined to less than 600,000 in 1978. In the United States the population of 14 to 24 year olds was only 27.4 million in 1960. It rose by 48.5 percent to 40.6 million in the following decade, and by a further 11.4 percent to 45 million in 1980. By 1990 the total will have dropped over 10 percent to 37.9 million. The increase in young people entering the labor market in the early 1980s was not offset by a corresponding increase in retirements, since the generation reaching retirement was born during the First World War and its immediate aftermath, when birth rates were exceptionally low. Adding yet further to this rare concurrence of demographic movements affecting the supply of labor was the sweeping social change in the attitude of women toward paid employment. The participation of women aged 25 to 54, and particularly of married women, has risen in all OECD countries since 1953, most spectacularly in the United States, Canada and Sweden. In the United States two-thirds of women now work in paid employment, compared to under two-fifths a generation ago. There has been a slight decline in male participation in the formal labor market, especially among young men, which probably reflects longer full-time education, but it has not been enough to offset the much larger increase in women seeking employment.

Patterns of Unemployment. North America shares with Western Europe a similar pattern of sex- and age-related unemployment. Women have slightly higher rates of unemployment than men. During the recession, however, the gap in Western Europe has narrowed, and in the United States it has been reversed. But the discrepancy between the male and female unemployment rate is insignificant as compared to the discrepancy between young people and prime-age adults.

Unemployment among young people aged 15 to 24 is two and a half to three times that of older workers. The most spectacular discrepancies occur in the least stable European democracies—Portugal, Spain, Italy, Turkey and, exceptionally, in Norway. The slight easing of demographic pressures has brought an improvement in the youth to adult unemployment ratios in most Western countries. The main reason, however, for better ratios is the deliberate adoption of measures to remove young people from the labor market such as apprenticeship schemes (Germany, Austria); keeping them in school longer (the United States); and planned school-to-work transition, including training and work experience (Denmark, Great Britain, France), which is sometimes combined with a guarantee of a place for any unemployed school-leaver. Despite these measures, nearly one in three of the OECD's unemployed is 24 years old or younger. In some countries two-fifths of young people are out of work, and among the unskilled and ethnic minorities, the figures may be half or more.

But in two other important respects patterns of unemployment diverge sharply between North America and Europe. The United

States has an intractable problem of black unemployment and, more specifically, of black youth unemployment. In 1979, estimates prepared for the OECD Review Team showed unemployment among young black men aged 16 to 19 running at four times that of young white men, and for young black women at six to seven times that of young white women. Other OECD countries have serious, though less spectacular problems, in finding employment for young people without skills or educational qualifications—what the Danes call the *Restgruppe*. Employers often prefer a married woman to an inexperienced school-leaver, although equal pay makes such women employees less economically attractive to employers. Those who combine all the disadvantages—being young, unskilled, unqualified and black—are the hopeless core of a deprived generation. They are the "lost generation" of the baby boom years who went from overcrowded schools to an overcrowded job market, and who are now being overtaken by their better-trained juniors. These unwanted 18 to 25 year olds present serious social problems manifested by high crime rates and an increase in drug addiction. Little thought has been given to how this group might be reabsorbed into the economy.

European OECD countries have to cope with racial discrimination in employment directed largely at recent immigrants. Black youth unemployment is high in the United Kingdom and in France, and Turkish youth unemployment is significant in West Germany. But ethic minorities are new to these European countries. Immigration has almost stopped now in the case of Great Britain. France and West Germany have actually reversed it, sending thousands of immigrants and "guest-workers" home. In practice, unemployment has been exported back to much poorer countries like Algeria and Turkey. The destabilizing consequences of thousands more unemployed young men, many of them with a taste for Western material goods, have not yet been seen. At the very least, some of the young unemployed will go into the drug trade seeking to make money by using their contacts in Western Europe. Others will be raw material for anti-Western organizations, and there are plenty of those in the Islamic world.

The United States has a long, lightly patrolled border with Mexico and has attracted millions of illegal immigrants from Central and Latin America. Figures for the United States vary from 4 million to 14 million. What is certain is that hunger and chaos in many Latin countries will drive millions more to attempt to emigrate. The United States has a nasty choice between draconian protection of its beaches and borders, hardly compatible with a humane society; absorbing millions of incomers when unemployment is still high; or providing investment, credit and aid on a scale massive enough to allow these developing countries the prospect of raising their living standards.

Duration. Unemployment problems diverge between Western Europe and North America in one other respect: North American unemployment is of much shorter duration. Whether Americans are more mobile or more enterprising, individuals (with the major exception already mentioned) do not stay unemployed for long. Over half of Great Britain's unemployed, and nearly two-thirds of France's, have been out of work for six months or more. In the United States, as in Scandinavia, the proportion is less than one-fifth. The Scandinavians have employment policies specifically tailored to the long-term unemployed. The North Americans move in and out of work, with opportunities for work increasing during cyclical upswings amd decreasing in a recession. The apathy and sullen despair of the long-term unemployed, many of them young, are more isolated phenomena in North America. If the United States already possesses an underclass in its inner city black males, then Europe is now busily creating one.

The high level of trade union organization in Europe means that the protection of existing jobs has taken precedence over the creation of new ones. Legal restrictions on dismissal and the right to redundancy payments, quite substantial for the long-term service worker, make non-recruitment and natural wastage the easiest ways to reduce the labor force. This sounds humane. In practice, however, it means that job holding becomes a quasi-monopoly, and that unemployment is concentrated on those who have not yet joined the labor market (the young) or are only loosely attached to it (unorganized workers in low paying jobs, married women).

Social and Political Consequences

The traditional blue-collar working class, which represented the majority of the work force in Europe until a few years ago, is being replaced by a much more diverse work force with little sense of class solidarity. The steady 25-year decline of the Labour vote in Great Britain and the erosion of the communist vote in France are among the political consequences of this far-reaching social change. Fewer and fewer voters describe themselves as working class. The old sense of a common bond of misery between unemployed people and employed blue collar workers with poor wages, sharing a similar life-style, has virtually disappeared. The employed in Europe continue to get richer; indeed, unlike those in the United States, their real wages continued to increase throughout the 1970s and into the 1980s, albeit more slowly than in the 1960s. The unemployed however have become poorer. In the last five years benefits have been reduced in several countries; in Great Britain, the earnings-related benefit was removed in 1982. So the gap, economically and psychologically, has widened between the employed and the unemployed.

In Europe, with so large a proportion of the unemployed being long term—one-third to two-fifths of the total number out of work—the specter of an embittered minority left out of society is becoming real. But these men and women, many of them young, are not so far the stuff of revolution; apathy rather than anger characterizes them, and their plight does not outrage the employed majority, even though unemployment is often named as the most serious issue of domestic politics. One reason for this is given above: the different material experiences of the employed and the unemployed, which make the employed defenders of their jobs and resistant to plans for work sharing and redistribution of work. The second reason is the belief that nothing can be done anyway; if the market does not provide jobs, no one else can. This negativism characterizes the unemployed as well as the employed. In a 1982 *Economist* survey on unemployed people in Great Britain, over half responded that nothing could be done to provide jobs for them.[6] The third reason is the cult of toughness that pervades contemporary politics. The comfortable majority persuade themselves that the unemployed are lazy ("they don't want to work"),

---

[6] "Jobless Too Placid," *The Economist*, December 4, 1982, p. 30.

greedy ("they want too much pay"), or feckless ("they've got no sense of responsibility").

Political leaders, protected and guarded from threatened terrorist acts, inevitably become remote from the daily lives of their people, and particularly from the lives of the poor and deprived. The age of the open-air mass meeting, addressed by Lloyd George in the Welsh villages or Clement Attlee in the East End of London, has given way to closely controlled television press conferences or at best meetings with invited audiences or carefully planned visits to successful factories. The image matters more than the words, and both matter more than the reality. Few television programs scrutinize the plight of the unemployed, or the despair of whole districts ruined when their company closed down. The employed do not want to be told about the problems of the unemployed, and they, after all, are the audience advertisers pursue. Even in democracies political leaders no longer learn from their own five senses the despair of unemployment and the misery of poverty. One is reminded of Field Marshal Haig's reaction when he saw the trenches in Flanders during the First World War: "Did we send men into that?"

Occasionally there is a local explosion of anger: Watts in California, Toxteth and Moss Side in the northwest of England, the steel making cities of Lorraine. Governments are stirred into action for a while, private employers are encouraged to start new businesses or training schemes, and public funds are found for job creation programs. Some experiments have been notably successful. For example, cooperation between the private industry council and the city has attracted many new jobs to Baltimore. "Fullemploy," a voluntary organization in Great Britain, has trained unqualified young people, many of them black, in information technology and has combined the training with tutorial support and pastoral care. Almost all its alumni have found permanent jobs. Ambitious national schemes have been tried as well: a job guarantee for the long-term unemployed in certain Scandinavian countries; a one-year Youth Training Scheme with places planned for 460,000 16 and 17 year olds in the United Kingdom. But full employment—a real job for everyone who wants to work—remains elusive.

Among unemployed workers, the unqualified, or those with obsolete skills, are particularly difficult to place—and this is true even before the full impact of the new information technologies is felt in our economies. Whatever the net effect of these new technologies on jobs—and there will be massive job creation alongside massive job destruction—the one certainty is that those with flexible skills and a broad education will be the best placed. Those without will carry the additional burden of being information-poor and will become further alienated from an increasingly uncomprehending society.

Nations pay a heavy price for mass unemployment, for unemployment benefits are a burden on public expenditure. In Great Britain, for instance, unemployment benefits together with the loss of tax revenues and social security contributions rose from $7.4 billion in 1978-79 to $23.7 billion in 1982-83 (at constant prices) and are the major reason why public expenditure as a share of gross national product has actually increased from 41 percent (1978-79) to 44 percent (1982-83) under a government committed to reducing it. They also explain why taxes in Great Britain, under Prime Minister Margaret Thatcher, have increased faster than in all but two other Western countries, Ireland and Italy, since 1979. Second, the unemployed move into the unoffical economy, picking up work on a cash or barter basis. It is estimated that Italy's unoffical economy produces the equivalent of 20 percent or more of the offical GNP, thus undermining society's capacity to finance welfare benefits and other public expenditure through taxes and social security contributions. Third, some young people drift into crime. The House of Lords Select Committee on Employment estimated in May 1982 that, for every 10,000 additional unemployed, 1,000 were charged with offenses and 56 ended up in prison. The higher cost of maintaining law and order has to be taken into account.

Consequences for the Free World

But perhaps the most serious—and the least tangible—consequence of mass unemployment is the effect on the standing and reputation of the free world. The staggering achievement of the democracies in the three postwar decades was to treble the standard of living of the ordinary man or woman; to provide enough jobs and good wages; and to offer an extensive system of benefits and pensions giving security in sickness and old age. The mass of the people, far from being a miserable proletariat, as Karl Marx predicted, were triumphantly enriched. That achievement nullified the appeal of communism in the West and attracted the new generation in the Soviet bloc itself. No war fought against a communist enemy in Vietnam, or Yemen, or Cuba has won the hearts and the minds of the people; but Western economic success, within the political context of democracy, managed to do that. The mixed economy and the welfare state proved to be just what ordinary people wanted.

Now that achievement is at risk. Unemployment in Western Europe is expected to continue at one in ten or one in eight for some years to come, even assuming the U.S. recovery is not slowed down after the 1984 election. Poverty is increasing: the diseases of malnutrition, like rickets, are beginning to reappear. Several million families and two and a half million children in Great Britain, for example, live below the offical poverty line. Benefits in most European countries are likely to be cut further, and as in the United States, the unemployed and single-parent families will lose most. The attractiveness of concentrating benefits on the poor through forms of negative income tax, or basic benefits financed by the withdrawal of tax allowances, is great. But as ever, the political price is high, since middle-income groups have, as in the United States, been the major net beneficiaries of the welfare state through pensions, education and health care. For the time being, the prospect is a deepening of the poverty of the poor.

III. Some Thoughts on Solutions

Microeconomic Remedies

Modest growth will not suffice by itself to bring unemployment down, although it is a prerequisite for doing so. Because European unemployment is made worse by the institutional and structural rigidities described above, the solutions must tackle those rigidities as well.

I do not believe the answers lie in a head-on attack on wage levels or the trade unions. Ralf Dahrendorf once said that the explanation for Great Britain's economic weakness lay in her culture, a culture that admires thinkers and academics and despises doers, the vocational and practical. But equally a head-on attack on the European educational system will not yield rapid dividends. Structural employment policies must be sensitive to the different sectors of the economy, to their power structures and their needs. They must be complemented by policies outside the economic area that deal with such problems as freedom of information, without which Europe's adoption of information technology will be hampered by the pervasive secrecy of its bureaucracies, and the recognition of vocational and practical achievements, as well as academic ones, for academic credit. (Examinations are the crucial gateways to higher education in Europe.)

The various sectors of the West European economy require a different approach if they are to yield the maximum number of permanent real jobs. What is dangerous in an industrial policy is to prop up obsolescent or dying industries in the name of saving jobs. It is expensive in the end and usually leads to protection against competition. There are more satisfactory and less expensive ways to create and maintain jobs.

In *industries producing internationally traded goods,* the most important contribution to creating jobs lies in the rapid dissemination of technological knowledge, the development of flexible modern training schemes, and the education of young people in basic information technology skills. There is unlikely to be a net gain in jobs, but jobs will be lost if there is not an adequate supply of skilled people at every level, from post-doctoral to post-basic training. Many youngsters who dislike school take to information technology like ducks to water.

In *traditional smokestack industries,* we should modernize what we can and stop supporting what we cannot. Money spent on sustaining obsolescent industries is money wasted. It is less expensive to pay retraining and removal expenses for employees or to help them set up in their own small businesses or cooperatives. Worst of all is to keep obsolescent industries going by proctecting them, except perhaps for a very short period to allow restructuring to take place.

In *traditional service industries* many jobs can be created, because this sector is labor-intensive and parts of it, such as construction, enter little into international trade. Creating jobs in the economic infrastructure by rehabilitating houses; by building and improving roads, bridges and sewers; by encouraging neighborhood energy conservation and environmental improvement schemes; and by recycling materials is relatively inexpensive in terms of capital investment per job. It is also unlikely to be inflationary because the small firms involved, and their unions, have little influence on prices or wages. Furthermore, infrastructure schemes (which are usually publicly funded to start with) actually pay for themselves over three or four years, especially if unemployment benefits are taken into account.

The energy-intensive, capital-intensive approach to the *primary industries* may be leading up an expensive blind alley. Such techniques seem increasingly destructive of the environment and of jobs and livelihoods in the Third World, as the experience of Brazil and the Shah's Iran both demonstrated. Sustainable techniques of organic farming, replanting of woodlands and hedges, preservation of wild species of animals and plants are vital to the long-term health of the planet and to its ability to sustain its population over time. Opportunities for jobs, particularly community service jobs, are considerable.

In the *public services*, there is plenty of work to be done, especially in health care and personal social services, but the crisis over public expenditure makes governments feel unable to finance them. It is unlikely therefore that public service jobs will increase much, unless wages fall or people are employed part time or as trainees.

The final sector, known in Europe as the *third sector* or the *associative sector*, is the most vigorous. Characterized by small firms of all kinds, it flourishes between the public and the private sectors, sometimes combining elements from both. It ranges at one end from workers' cooperatives to, at the other end, small private businesses financed by capitalized unemployment benefits. It includes enterprise trusts in Great Britain and *boutiques de gestion* in France, both of which are networks of advisers, comprised of local authorities and businessmen who attempt to help new businesses survive. Third sector firms draw on public funds for loan guarantees, grants for feasibility studies, and low-interest loans; they draw on private funds for venture capital. Tens of thousands of jobs have been created at low cost in the tertiary sector, which is largely outside the formal corporative structure of big industry and big labor. Many third sector firms live in niches in large mass production markets or innovate their way into creating a new market. Microelectronics, because it is cheap in capital terms and adaptable to batch and customized production, should help the third sector. Indeed, it is one of the best hopes in Europe for varied and exciting employment.

Sectoral approaches apart, unemployment can be brought down by reducing the supply of labor. Among the most promising possibilities is to *delay entry into working life* by extending education and training. European young people start formal work much younger than do Americans. Provision of training in vocational and social skills, combined with work experience, could delay entry for most youth up to the age of 18 and provide them with time to learn skills essential to tomorrow's society.

Some other approaches that warrant serious consideration are:

Job sharing. Two young people share a real job and spend the other half of their time in training. This doubles the number of young people with the hands-on experience that so many firms demand. It also solves the problem of high youth pay since each young person is paid half a full wage plus half a training allowance. The firm benefits from flexibility—it can easily ask for extra work hours for a rush order—and from the reduction of absenteeism or disruption due to sickness. Job sharing is also useful for people with family responsibilities.

Flexible Retirement. Early retirement has taken many thousands of workers out of the labor force, but some have taken other jobs. The usual condition is that they must be replaced by an unemployed person. Partial retirement is very attractive to many older people. It means that hours can gradually be reduced; such a person might share a job with a young worker whose hours could be gradually increased. The great obstacle to this is pension scheme rules; they will need to be relaxed if phased retirement is to become more generally available.

Reduction in Hours of Work. A reduction in hours has to be large—ten percent or more—to create job opportunites. A West

German proposal is that employers and workers share the reduced earnings, say ten percent between them, while the government subsidizes half the cost of additional workers up to ten percent of the total work force. Unit costs would remain the same, the employer would pay no more, the work force would lose five percent of its pay but would reduce its working hours by ten percent, and savings in unemployment benefits would enable the government to meet the cost of subsidizing the additional workers.

In his book, *The Great Transformation*, Karl Polyani wrote of the Industrial Revolution that "the common sense attitude towards change was discarded in favor of a mystical readiness to accept the social consequences of economic improvement, whatever they might be."[7] So powerful has been that mystique that it is rarely asked if the adoption of a particular process or technology will actually add to the happiness and contentment of mankind. Yet if one starts from the assumption that people do not exist to serve technology, but that technology exists to serve people, one has already gone a long way toward an employment policy.

Modern Western governments, and those in the Soviet bloc too, have become enslaved by the industrial process. In its name corporate structures of great rigidity have been devised and economies of scale have been pursued regardless of the effect on the quality of life. Industrial societies have paid the price in loss of commitment to work, in strained industrial relations, and in social antagonism. But the momentum has gone even further. Governments have artificially made capital cheap and labor expensive, subsidizing the former and taxing the latter. Graduate engineers and managers have been trained in technology and finance but not sufficiently in human management, so that most of them prefer working with machines to working with people. Efficiency is measured, not by the value added to all the inputs of production, but to one input—labor.

In Europe there is evidence in some industries that capital productivity has fallen more than labor productivity has risen. Public money is poured into depressed regions without any direct reference to the number of jobs created. Governments favor manufacturing and large corporations—indeed grants and tax allowances

---

[7] *The Great Tranformation*, New York: Rinehart, 1944.

are often limited to investment in manufacturing and processing and to companies above a certain size. These criteria mean that jobs are unnecessarily expensive to create. Far more jobs could be created in construction, civil engineering, and small businesses for the same amount of public money. The cost per job in house modernization, civil engineering and domestic energy conservation is estimated at only $3,700 to $8,800 in the United Kingdom, little different from the overall cost of keeping someone unemployed. By contrast, jobs in the car industry cost $44,000 to $148,000 per job.

Macroeconomic Remedies

Shonfield argues that Western governments have never succeeded in coordinating their economic policies. They failed to agree on a response to the 1973 oil shock; they failed to avoid the 1975 slump; they failed to support President Carter's 1976 recovery program; and they succeeded, just once, but without any agreement, in all deflating together in 1979, bringing about a much more savage recession than any one government really intended.[8] Now they cannot agree on how to recover. The harsh truth is that the West has not pulled itself together since the United States effectively lost its economic hegemony in the 1960s.

The disagreements within the Western Alliance are ideological as well as geographic. In 1981 and 1982, the government of France floated initiatives for European employment programs and for ambitious international initiatives in technology transfer. It received support from some other nations, but never enough to outweigh the opposition of conservative governments in Washington, London and, more recently, Bonn. The strains within the European Economic Community, especially on agricultural policy and on the question of contributions to and benefits from the EEC budget, have obsessed member governments to the point where wider macroeconomic policies have little chance of being pursued. The EEC lurches from crisis to crisis wasting its energies on immediate problems, neglecting long-term strategies. One recent success of Community economic policy, however, is the European Monetary

---

[8] *Op. cit.*, pp. 58-59.

System (EMS), which has modified the movements of individual European currencies and given support to currencies under pressure. Great Britain, however, is not a member. The EEC has also established a useful bargaining position on international economic bodies like GATT and the Multi-Fiber Agreement. But it cannot develop further without coordinating separate national economic policies. Despite the clear evidence that international factors—such as currency movements and interest rates reflecting world financial opinion, world recession or growth, political events like the Gulf war—far outweigh the impact of purely national policy-making, European governments cling persistently to the illusion of national economic sovereignty.

Clear consultation within the EEC—not only on economic questions, but on foreign policy and defense issues—would be a step in the right direction. Indeed, the political secretariat needs to be developed so that ministers can be briefed and serviced from a Community as well as a national source. An expanded EEC budget, made possible by an increase in "own resources"—now limited to one percent of value-added taxes—would enable the social and regional funds to be more generously financed. The EEC could also build on its current research into information technology, the so-called European Strategic Program of Research and Development in Information Technology (ESPRIT), to encourage sunrise industries and create a European industrial policy. The new technologies disregard frontiers; many already operate in the international market. But the EEC, in spite of a GNP almost as great as that of the United States, has only recently begun to discuss common regulations and a common public purchasing policy in telecommunications and in computer software.

In Japan there is no great enthusiasm for the thankless job of political leadership in dealing with international economic issues; it devotes its energies to establishing a commanding lead in export markets and advanced technology. The United States therefore remains the only leader the West has, yet its economic power no longer justifies a hegemonic role. Former U.S. Secretary of State Henry Kissinger recently proposed a radical devolution of power and responsibility to the Europeans within NATO.[9] His proposal should have an economic analogue.

---

[9] "A Plan to Reshape NATO," *Time*, March 5, 1984, pp. 20-24.

The present U.S. economic balance between an expansionary, even profligate, fiscal policy and a cautious monetary one is inherently unstable. True, the dollar has come down a bit, and the economy is still growing fast; but so is the current-account deficit, estimated at $38 billion in 1983 by the U.S. Department of Commerce. Interest rates have remained high to attract capital from overseas and to safeguard the dollar, but they discourage investment and weaken the recovery. It seems highly probable that the U.S. government will have to move after the presidential election to cut the budget deficits, thus bringing interest rates down. Such action by the federal government would leave room for other Western governments to adopt more expansionary policies, and they should be encouraged to do so. It is in no one's interest to see the current recovery fade.

Complementarity between the economic policies of Western governments and Japan implies greater coordination. Within the EEC, the EMS has helped to bring that about and has modified sharp currency fluctuations that can devastate industry, especially the exporting industry, as the experience of the United Kingdom from 1979 to 1982, and of the United States now, so clearly shows. Cooperation between governments and national banks within the OECD could moderate the serious repercussions of floating rates. Indeed, as economists at Stanford University proposed last year, the ideal recipe for greater economic stability would be one in which the Western country, or region, with the strongest currency would expand it and would hand over responsibility for acting as an engine for growth to one of the other Western nations when its own currency came under pressure. This way no economy would overheat. The OECD is probably the only acceptable mechanism for bringing about coordination, and this has now been made easier by the convergence of inflation rates and growth rates among OECD countries.

With respect to the Third World, a hopeful sign is the emergence of fresh initiatives on aid and lending to the developing countries. Their recovery is an essential element in sustaining steady international growth. Western governments and Western banks have been compelled, by the threat of a catastrophe, to put together rescue packages and to reschedule debt. The international organizations—the International Monetary Fund (IMF), the World

Bank, the IDA—have suffered grievously from the paucity of their resources at a time when a stimulus to economic development in the Third World would make a great deal of sense. The irony is acute, for at the present time, money is flowing into the United States from debt-ridden developing countries, some of it in the form of interest for capital repayments to U.S. banks, some of it capital looking for a safe haven. The World Bank estimated the net inflow from South to North, short-term investments apart, to be $11 billion in 1983.[10] The Reagan Administration's economic policies have contributed to the burdens that beggar the Third World, yet the Administration opposes any increase in contributions to the international bodies that enable those burdens to be carried.

Here too, some rethinking has occurred. Faced with the U.S. government's decision to limit its contribution to the IDA to $750 million a year, the French and British governments offered to contribute to a supplementary fund. Both took the view that a decline in low-interest loans to the world's poorest countries was contrary to the long-term interests of the Western Alliance. Indeed, the case for expanding low-interest loans and special drawing rights to the non-oil producing Third World countries is very strong. Tragically, only those countries directly threatened by left-wing guerrilla movements, like El Salvador, seem to open the purse strings of the U.S. federal treasury. The West European governments and Japan, less pressured by frequent electioneering, should take the lead in negotiating a new North-South economic relationship. This should include a code of practice covering relations between governments and multinational corporations and the creation of processing industries for raw materials in developing countries themselves.

The Atlantic Alliance has lost its primacy in American eyes because of the rapid development of the Pacific Basin countries, now more important trading partners to the United States than Western Europe. The vision of a two-pillar Alliance has faded because of Western Europe's inability to pull itself together. Technologically Europe has lost ground to Japan and the newly industrializing Asian countries. Yet the Atlantic Alliance remains the

---

[10] "Beggaring the Poor," *The Economist*, February 18, 1984, p. 15.

core of the West's defense and the heart of the political system that links together countries committed to individual freedom. Fragmented policies have not succeeded in coping with the oil shocks or with the world recession. Has the time come for a new effort to construct political responses capable of matching the problems of our time? The institutions exist—the OECD, GATT, the IMF, and the EEC. What is required are politicians with the purpose and the will.